Guitar Chord Songbook

Early Rock

ISBN 978-1-4234-2375-1

HAL•LEONARD®
CORPORATION
7777 W. BLUEMOUND RD. P.O. BOX 13819 MILWAUKEE, WI 53213

Visit Hal Leonard Online at
www.halleonard.com

Guitar Chord Songbook

Contents

All Alone Am I

English Lyric by Arthur Altman
Original Lyric by Jean Ioannidis
Music by M. Hadjidakis

All a - lone am I,   ev-er since you

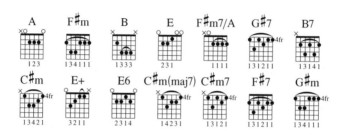

Chorus 1

        A   F#m B   E
All a - lone am I, ever since you good - bye.

    F#m   F#m7/A   G#7
All a - lone with just the beat of my heart.

        A   F#m   B   E
People all a - round, but I don't hear a sound,

       F#m B7   E
Just the lonely beating of ___ my heart.

Verse 1

     E   B7
    No use in holding other hands, for I'd be holding only emptiness.

  C#m   G#7
    No use in kissing other lips, for I'd be thinking just of your caress.

Chorus 2   *Repeat Chorus 1*

Verse 2

Spoken: *No other voice can say the words*

E   E+   E6   E   E6

F#m   B   C#m   C#m(maj7)   C#m7

My heart must hear to ever sing again.

The words you used to whisper low,

F#7   B7

No other love can ever bring again.

Chorus 3

A   F#m   B   E

All a - lone am I, ever since you good - bye.

F#m   F#m7/A   G#7

All a - lone with just the beat of my heart.

A   F#m   B   E

People all a - round, but I don't hear a sound,

F#m   B7   N.C.   E   A   G#m   A   B   E

Just the lonely beating of my heart.

All I Have to Do Is Dream

Words and Music by
Boudleaux Bryant

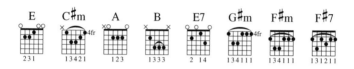

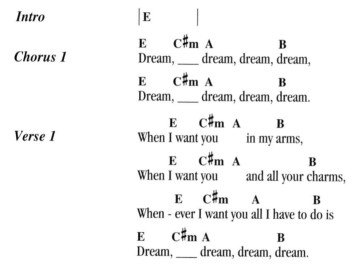

Intro

|E |

Chorus 1

  E   C#m A   B
Dream, ___ dream, dream, dream,

  E   C#m A   B
Dream, ___ dream, dream, dream.

Verse 1

     E   C#m A   B
When I want you   in my arms,

      E   C#m A   B
When I want you   and all your charms,

       E C#m   A   B
When - ever I want you all I have to do is

  E   C#m A   B
Dream, ___ dream, dream, dream.

Verse 2

       E   C#m A   B
When I feel blue ___ in the night,

       E   C#m A   B
And I need you   to hold me tight,

          E   C#m   A   B   E A E E7
When - ever I want you all I have to do is dream.

Bridge 1

   A   G#m
I can make you mine, taste your lips of wine,

   F#m   B   E   E7
Anytime,   night or day.

   A   G#m   F#7   B
Only trouble is,   gee whiz, I'm dreaming my life a - way.

Verse 3

      E   C#m A   B
I need you so,   that I could die.

      E   C#m A   B
I love you so,   and that is why,

        E   C#m   A   B
When - ever I want you all I have to do is…

Chorus 2

   E   C#m A   B
Dream, ___ dream, dream, dream,

   E   A E E7
Dream.

Bridge 2   *Repeat Bridge 1*

Verse 4   *Repeat Verse 3*

Outro   *Repeat Chorus 1 till fade*

Are You Sincere

Words and Music by
Wayne Walker and Lucky Moeller

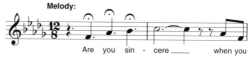

Melody:

Are you sin - cere _____ when you

(Capo 1st fret)

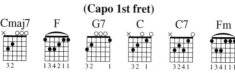

Cmaj7   F   G7   C   C7   Fm

Verse 1

N.C.   Cmaj7   F   G7
Are you sin - cere when you say, "I love you?"

Cmaj7   F   G7
Are you sin - cere when you say, "I'll be true?"

C   C7   F
Do you mean ev'ry word that my ears have heard?

C   G7
I'd like to know which way to go, will our love grow?

C   F   C
Are you sin - cere? (Are you sin - cere?)

Verse 2

N.C.   Cmaj7   F   G7   F   G7
Are you sin - cere when you say you miss me? (You miss me.)

Cmaj7 F   G7   F   G7
Are you sin - cere ev'ry time you kiss me? (You kiss me.)

C   C7   F
And are you really mine ev'ry day, all the time?

C   G7
I'd like to know which way to go, will our love grow?

C   F   C   N.C.
Are you sin - cere? (Are you sin - cere?)

Interlude

| Cmaj7   F | G7 | |

Outro

C   C7   F   Fm
Are you really mine ev'ry day, all the time?

F   C
I'd like to know (I'd like to know.) which way to go, (Which way to go.)

G7   N.C.
Will our love grow? (Will our love grow?)

C   F   C
Are you sin - cere? (Are you sin - cere?)

Be True to Your School

Words and Music by
Brian Wilson and Mike Love

Melody:

When some loud brag-gart tries to put me down, _

(Capo 3rd fret)

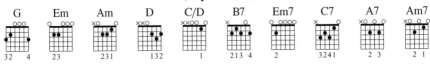

G   Em   Am   D   C/D   B7   Em7   C7   A7   Am7

Intro

         G
When some loud braggart

           Em
Tries to put me down,

           Am
And says his school is great,

D
  I tell him right away,

         G
"Now, what's the matter, buddy,

           Em
Ain't you heard of my school?

          Am   **D**   **C/D**   **D**
It's number one in the state."

Chorus 1

         C/D   **G**
So be __ true to your school __ now,

                   B7
Just like you would to your girl ___ or guy.

             Em7
Be true to your school ___ now

             C7
And let your colors fly.

A7   **Am7** **D** **C/D** **D** **C/D**
  Be true to your school.

Verse 1

```
                    G
I got a letterman sweater

            Em7
With the letter in front

              Am7
I got for football and track.

                  D
I'm proud to wear it.

              G
Now, when I cruise around

            Em7
The other parts of the town,

              Am7
I got a decal in back.
```

Chorus 2

```
            D                 G
So be true to your school __ now,

                             B7
Just like you would to your girl __ or guy.

                    Em7
Be true to your school ____ now

                    C7
And let your colors fly.

A7                      Am7
  Be true to your school.
```

| D   C/D | D   C/D |

Verse 2

        G
Come Friday, we'll be jacked up

        Em7
On the football game,

        Am7
And I'll be ready to fight.

        D
We're gonna smash 'em now.

        G
My girly will be working

        Em7
On her pompoms now,

        Am7
And she'll be yelling tonight.

Chorus 3

        D   **G**
So be true to your school __ now,

        B7
Just like you would to your girl __ or guy.

        Em7
Be true to your school __ now,

        C7
And let your colors fly.

A7   **Am7**
  Be true to your school.

 | **D**   **C/D** | **D**   **C/D** |

Outro

      G   **Em7**
‖: Ra, ra, ra, be true to your school.

Am7   **D**
Ra, ra, ra, be true to your school. :‖ *Repeat and fade*

At My Front Door

Words and Music by
John C. Moore and Ewart G. Abner, Jr.

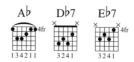

Intro

| A♭ | | | | | | | |

Chorus 1

A♭
Crazy little mama come knocking,

Was a knocking at my front door, door, door.

D♭7   A♭
Crazy little mama come knocking, knocking at my front door.

  E♭7   D♭7
Cra - zy little mama come knock, knock, knocking

    A♭
Just ____ like she did before.

Verse 1

  A♭
I woke up this morning with a feeling of despair,

Lookin' for my baby, and she wasn't there.

    D♭7
Heard ____ someone knockin', and much to my surprise,

    A♭
There ____ stood my baby, lookin' in my eyes.

E♭7   D♭7
Crazy little mama come knock, knock, knocking

    A♭
Just ____ like she did before.

Verse 2

       A♭
If you got a little mama and you wanna keep her neat,

Keep your little mama off my street.

       D♭7
Same ___ thing 'ill happen like it did before,

         A♭
She'll come knock, knock, knocking at my door.

E♭7   D♭7
Crazy little mama come knock, knock, knocking

      A♭
Just ___ like she did before.

Chorus 2   *Repeat Chorus 1*

      N.C.(A♭)
Bridge   A-womp, a-womp, a-didaly womp,

A-womp, womp, didaly womp, a-womp, womp.

Sax Solo | D♭7 | | A♭ | |
                | E♭7 | D♭7 | A♭ | |

            A♭ N.C.   A♭ N.C.
Verse 3   If you got a little mama and you wanna keep her neat,

           A♭ N.C.
Keep your little mama off my street.

D♭7 N.C.   D♭7 N.C.
Same thing will happen like it did   before,

       A♭ N.C.
She'll come knock, knock, knocking at my door.

E♭7   D♭7
Crazy little mama come knock, knock, knocking

      A♭
Just ___ like she did before.

Verse 4   *Repeat Verse 1 w/ vocal ad lib.*

Verse 5   *Repeat Verse 1 w/ vocal ad lib.*

Outro | A♭ | | | |
              | D♭7 | | A♭ | |
              | E♭7 | D♭7 | A♭ | |

Big Girls Don't Cry

Words and Music by
Bob Crewe and Bob Gaudio

Melody:

Big girls don't cry.

G   D   C   D7   E7   Am7   A7

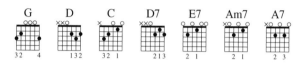

Intro

N.C.(G) (D)   (C) (D7)
‖: Big   girls   don't cry.   :‖

|G   E7 |Am7 D7 |

Chorus 1

G E7 Am7 D7   G   E7 Am7   D7
(Big girls)   Don't cry, ___ (They don't cry.)

G E7 Am7 D7   G   E7 Am7   D7
Big girls   don't cry. (Who said they don't cry?)

Verse 1

G E7 Am7 D7   G E7 Am7   D7
My girl   said good - bye. (My, oh, my.)

G E7 Am7 D7   G   C   G N.C.
My girl   didn't cry. (I wonder why.)

Bridge 1

E7
(Silly boy.) Told my girl we had to break up,

A7
(Silly boy.) Thought that she would call my bluff.

D7
(Silly boy.) Then she said to my surprise,

G   D   C   D7
Big girls don't cry.

Chorus 2

G E7 Am7 D7 G   E7 Am7   D7
Big girls   don't cry. (They don't cry.)

G E7 Am7 D7 G   E7 Am7   D7
Big girls   don't cry. (Who said they don't cry?)

Trumpet Solo   ‖: G   E7 |Am7 D7 :‖

Verse 2

G E7 Am7 D7   G E7 Am7   D7
(Ba - by.)   I was cruel, ___ (I was cruel.)

G E7 Am7 D7 G   C   G   N.C.
Ba - by,   I'm a fool. (I'm such a fool.)

Bridge 2

          E7
(Silly girl.) Shame on you, your mama said,

          A7
(Silly girl.) Shame on you, you're cryin' in bed.

          D7
(Silly girl.) Shame on you, you told a lie.

G D   C D7
Big girls do cry.

Chorus 3

G E7 Am7 D7 G   E7 Am7   D7
(Big girls)   Don't cry, ___ (They don't cry.)

G E7 Am7 D7 G   E7   Am7 D7
Big girls   don't cry. (That's just an ali - bi.)

Outro

        G D   C   D7
‖: Big girls don't cry. :‖ *Repeat and fade*

The Big Hurt

Words and Music by
Wayne Shanklin

Melody:

Now it be - gins, _   now that you're

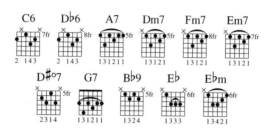

C6   Db6   A7   Dm7   Fm7   Em7

D#°7   G7   Bb9   Eb   Ebm

Intro | C6 | Db6 | C6 | Db6 |

Verse 1

    C6   Db6
    Now it begins,   now that you're gone,

    C6   Db6
    Needles and pins,   twilight till dawn.

    C6   A7 Dm7   Fm7
    Watching that clock   till you re - turn,

    Em7   D#°7 Dm7   G7
    Lighting that torch   and watching it burn.

Verse 2

C6   **D♭6**
Now it begins,   day after day.

C6   **D♭6**
This is my life   ticking away.

C6   **A7** **Dm7**   **Fm7**
Waiting to hear   footsteps that say

Em7   **D#°7 Dm7**   **G7**
Love will ap - pear   and this time to stay.

Bridge

B♭9   **E♭**
Oh, each time you go   I try to pretend.

E♭m   **G7**
It's over at last, this time the big hurt will end.

Verse 3

C6   **D♭6**
Now it begins,   now that you're gone,

C6   **D♭6**
Needles and pins   twilight till dawn.

C6   **A7** **Dm7**   **Fm7**
But if you don't   come back a - gain,

Em7   **D#°7 Dm7**   **G7**   **C6**
I wonder when,   oh, when will it end, the big hurt.

D♭6 **C6** **D♭6** **C6 D♭6 C6**
The big hurt. The big hurt.

Bird Dog

Words and Music by
Boudleaux Bryant

Melody:

John - ny   is   a   jok - er. ___ *Spoken: (He's a   bird.)*

(Capo 2nd fret)

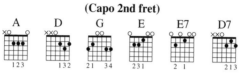

Intro	‖: A D G ‖ E :‖	

Verse 1

  A
Johnny is a joker. *Spoken: (He's a bird.)*

A very funny joker. (He's a bird.)

    D
But when he jokes my honey (He's a dog.)

    A
His jokin' ain't so funny. (What a dog.)

E7   **D7**
Johnny is the joker that's a tryin' to steal my baby.

           A   **D G E**
(He's a bird dog.)

Verse 2

  A
Johnny sings a love song. (Like a bird.)

Sings the sweetest love song. (You ever heard.)

    D
But when he sings to my gal (What a howl.)

    A
To me he's just a wolf dog. (On the prowl.)

E7   **D7**
Johnny wants to fly away and puppy love my baby.

           A   **D G E**
(He's a bird dog.)

Chorus 1

D7
Hey, bird dog, get away from my quail.

A
Hey, bird dog, you're on the wrong trail.

E7   **D7**   **A**
Bird dog, you'd better leave my   lovely dove a - lone.

D7
Hey, bird dog, get away from my chick.

A
Hey, bird dog, you better get away quick.

E7   **D7**   **A**   **D G E**
Bird dog, you better find a chicken little of your own.

| A   D   G | E |

Verse 3

A
Johnny kissed the teacher. (He's a bird.)

He tiptoed up to reach her. (He's a bird.)

    D
Well, he's the teacher's pet now. (He's a dog.)

    A
What he wants he can get now. (What a dog.)

   E7   **D7**
He even made the teacher let him sit next to my baby.

       A   **D G E**
(He's a bird dog.)

Chorus 2   *Repeat Chorus 1*

Outro ||: A   D G | E   :|| *Repeat and fade*

Black Denim Trousers and Motorcycle Boots

Words and Music by
Jerry Leiber and Mike Stoller

He wore black den-im trou-sers and   mo-tor-cy-cle boots

Cm   G7   Fm

Intro

| N.C. (Drums) | | | |
| Cm | | G7 | Cm | N.C. |

Chorus 1

        Cm   G7
He wore black denim trousers and motorcycle boots

                  Cm
And a black leather jacket with an eagle on the back.

            G7
He had a hopped up cycle that took off like a gun.

           Cm
That fool was the terror of Highway 101. (Doo, wha, doo, wha.)

Verse 1

        Cm   G7
Well, he never washed his face and he never combed his hair.

              Cm
He had axle grease embedded under - neath his fingernails.

          Fm
On the muscle of his arm was a red tattoo,

  G7   Cm
A picture of a heart saying, "Mother I love you."

            G7
He had a pretty girlfriend by the name of Mary Lou,

           Cm
But he treated her just like he treated all the rest.

             Fm
And ev'rybody pitied her 'cause ev'rybody knew

  G7   Cm
He loved that doggone motorcycle best.

Chorus 2

              Cm   G7
He wore black denim trousers and motorcycle boots

                        Cm
And a black leather jacket with an eagle on the back.

                   G7
He had a hopped up cycle that took off like a gun.

                Cm
That fool was the terror of Highway 101.

Interlude   ‖: Cm | | | :‖

Verse 2

              Cm   G7
Mary Lou, poor girl, she pleaded and she begged him not to leave.

                      Cm
She said, "I've got a feeling if you ride tonight I'll grieve."

                          Fm
But her tears were shed in vain, and her ev'ry word was lost

        G7   Cm
In the rumble of his engine and the smoke from his exhaust.

                   G7
He took off like a devil, there was fire in his eyes.

                      Cm
He said, "I'll go a thousand miles be - fore the sun can rise."

                      Fm
But he hit a screaming diesel that was California bound,

        G7   Cm
And when they cleared the wreckage all they found was his…

Chorus 3

           Cm   G7
Black denim trousers and motorcycle boots

                      Cm
And a black leather jacket with an eagle on the back.

                   G7
But they couldn't find the cycle that took off like a gun,

                      Cm
And they never found the terror of Highway 101.

Blue Velvet

Words and Music by
Bernie Wayne and Lee Morris

Melody:

She wore blue vel - vet,

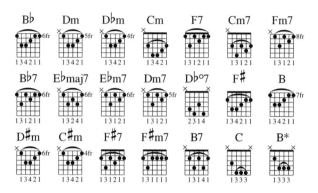

Intro

Bb Dm Dbm Cm F7
(Blue velvet. Whoa, whoa, ooh.)

Verse 1

Bb Dm Dbm Cm
She wore blue velvet, (Whoa, whoa.)

F7   Bb Dm Dbm Cm
Bluer than velvet was the night. (Whoa, whoa, whoa.)

F7   Bb Cm7 F7
Softer than satin was the light from the stars.

Bb Dm Dbm Cm
She wore blue velvet, (Whoa, whoa.)

F7   Bb Dm Dbm Cm
Bluer than velvet were her eyes. (Whoa, whoa, whoa.)

F7   Fm7 Bb7
Warmer than May, her ten - der sighs. Love was ours.

Bridge

E♭maj7   E♭m7
Ours, a love I held tightly,

B♭   B♭7
Feeling the rapture grow.

E♭maj7   E♭m7
Like a flame burning brightly.

Dm7   D♭°7 Cm7   F7
But when she left,   gone was the glow of…

Verse 2

B♭ Dm   D♭m Cm
Blue velvet. (Whoa, whoa.)

     F7   B♭   Dm D♭m Cm
But in my heart there'll always be, (Whoa, whoa, whoa.)

         F7   Fm7 B♭7
Precious and warm, a memory through the years.

E♭maj7   E♭m7   B♭   F♯
And I still can see blue velvet through my tears.

Verse 3

B D♯m Dm C♯m
She wore blue velvet, (Whoa, whoa.)

F♯7   B D♯m Dm C♯m
But in my heart there'll always be, (Whoa, whoa, whoa.)

     F♯7   F♯m7 B7
Precious and warm, a mem - ory through the years.

N.C.   B
And I still can see blue velvet through my tears.

D♯m Dm C♯m C B*
(Blue velvet. Ooh, ooh,   ooh, ooh.)

Blueberry Hill

Words and Music by Al Lewis,
Larry Stock and Vincent Rose

Melody:

I found my thrill ___   on ___ Blue-ber-ry

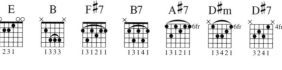

Intro | E | | B | | |

Verse 1
          E   **B**
I found my thrill ___ on Blueberry Hill,

       F#7   **B E B**
On Blueberry Hill ___ when I found you.

Verse 2
          E   **B**
The moon stood still ___ on Blueberry Hill

       F#7   **B E B**
And lingered until ___ my dream came true.

Bridge 1
    F#7   **B**   **E** **F#7**   **B B7**
The wind in the willow played love's sweet melo - dy.

    A#7   **D#m** **A#7**
But all of those vows you made

 D#m A#7 **D#7 F#7**
 Are never to be.

Verse 3
     B   **E**   **B**
Tho' we're apart, ___ you're part of me still.

         F#7   **B E B**
For you were my thrill ___ on Blueberry Hill.

Bridge 2
    F#7   **B**   **E** **F#7**   **B B7**
The wind in the willow played love's sweet melo - dy.

    A#7   **D#m** **A#7**
But all of those vows you made

 D#m **A#7** **D#7 F#7**
 Were only to be.

Outro   *Repeat Verse 3*

Do You Want to Dance?

Words and Music by
Bobby Freeman

Melody:

Well, do you wan-na dance and, a,

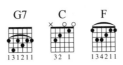

Intro

| N.C.(Drums) | | | |
| G7 | | | |

Verse 1
                          C   F
Well, do you wanna dance and, a, hold my hand?

C   F
Tell me, I'm your lover man.

C   F   C   F
Oh, baby,   do you want to dance?

Verse 2
                          C   F
Well, do you wanna dance and, a, make romance?

C   F
Squeeze me all through the night.

C   F   C   F
Oh, baby,   do you wanna dance?

Verse 3

          C   F
Well, do you wanna dance under the moonlight?

C   F
    Squeeze me, all through the night.

    C   F   C   F
Oh, baby,   do you wanna dance?

Guitar Solo

G7				
C	F	C	F	
C	F	G7		

Verse 4

               C   F
Well, do you wanna dance and, a, hold my hand?

C   F
    Squeeze me and say I'm your man.

    C   F   C   F
Oh,   baby,   do you wanna dance?

Verse 5

              C   F
Well, do you wanna dance under ___ the moonlight?

C   F
    Squeeze and kiss me, all through the night.

    C   F   C   F
Oh, baby,   do you wanna dance?

Verse 6

              C   F
Well, do you wanna dance and, a, make romance?

C   F
Kiss and squeeze me. Mm, yes.

C   F   C   F
Do you   wanna dance?

Interlude | G7 | | | | N.C. |
| | | G7 | | |

Verse 7
C   F
Well, do you wanna dance and, a, hold my hand?

C   F
Squeeze me and tell me I'm your lover man.

  C   F   C   G7
Oh, baby,   do you wanna dance?

Verse 8
              C   F
Well, do you wanna dance under ___ the moonlight?

C   F
  Squeeze and hug me, all through the night.

  C   F   C   G7
Oh, baby,   do you wanna dance?

Verse 9
         C   F
Well, do you, do you, do you, do you wanna dance?

C   F
Do you, do you, do you, do you wanna dance?

C   F   C G7
Do you, do you, do you, do you wanna dance?

| G7 | | | | C N.C. |

EARLY ROCK

27

Bluejean Bop

Words and Music by
Gene Vincent and Hal Levy

Melody:

Blue-jean ba-by, ___   with your

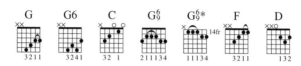

G   G6   C   G⁶₉   G⁶₉*   F   D

Intro

           G **G6**   **C**   **G⁶₈ G⁶₈***
Bluejean baby,   with your big blue eyes,

              G **G6**   **F C** **G⁶₈**
Don't want you lookin'   at oth - er guys.

                G **G6** **C**   **G⁶₈**
Got to make you give me   one ___ more chance.

N.C.
I can't keep still so, baby, let's dance.

Verse 1

             C
Well, the bluejean bop is the bop for me.

             G
Well, it's the bop that's done in dungaree.

         C
You dip your hip, free your knee,

G N.C.
Swing in on your heel, baby, one, two, three.

Chorus 1

             C   **G**
Well, the bluejean bop, bluejean bop, oh, baby, bluejean bop.

          D
Bluejean bop, oh, baby, bluejean bop,

                    G
Baby, won't you bop with Gene. ___ *Bop, Blue Caps, bop!*

Guitar Solo 1

G				
C		**G**		
D		**G**		

Verse 2   G
Well, bluejean baby, when I bop with you,

Well, my heart starts a-hoppin' like a, a kangaroo.

C
My feet do things they've never done before.

G N.C.
Well, a bluejean baby, give me more, more, more.

            C   G
Chorus 2   Well, the bluejean bop, bluejean bop, oh, baby, bluejean bop.

D
A, bluejean bop, oh, baby, bluejean bop,

                           G
Baby, won't you bop with Gene. ___ *Rock it again, Blue Caps, go!*

Guitar Solo 2   *Repeat Guitar Solo 1*

            C   G
Chorus 3   Well, the bluejean bop, bluejean bop, oh, baby, bluejean bop.

D
Bluejean bop, oh, baby, bluejean bop,

                           G
Baby, won't you bop with Gene. ___

Blue Caps, bop with Gene, now, let's go!

Guitar Solo 3 |G | |D |G |
                       | | | | |
                       |D | |G | |

                                G
Outro   Well, it's   a, bluejean, a, bluejean bop.

A, bluejean, a, bluejean bop, oh, baby,

C
  A, bluejean, a, bluejean bop.

G
  A, bluejean, a, bluejean bop,

D   G G$^6_9$
  A, bluejean, oh, baby, won't you bop with Gene.

Bobby's Girl

Words and Music by
Gary Klein and Henry Hoffman

Melody:

I know just   what   to   say, _

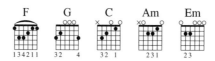

```
  F        G        C        Am       Em
```

Intro
```
            F              G
‖: (You're not a kid anymore.) :‖
```

Verse 1
```
                C                        Am
Spoken:  When people ask of me    what would you like to be,

F                        Em          F          G
  Now that you're not a kid   anymore?   (You're not a kid anymore.)

C                        Am
I know just what to say,    I answer right away.

F                        Em                    F  G  N.C.
There's just one thing I've been wishing for.
```

Chorus 1
```
                  C
I wanna be   Bobby's girl,

         Am
I wanna be   Bobby's girl.

F                            G    N.C.
That's the most important thing to me.

                  C
And if I was   Bobby's girl,

          F            G                   F      C
If I was   Bobby's girl, what a faithful, thankful girl ___ I'd be.
```

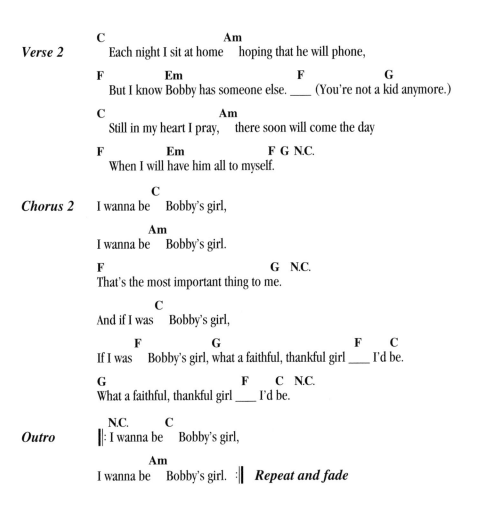

Verse 2
C   Am
Each night I sit at home   hoping that he will phone,

F   Em   F   G
But I know Bobby has someone else. ___ (You're not a kid anymore.)

C   Am
Still in my heart I pray,   there soon will come the day

F   Em   F G N.C.
When I will have him all to myself.

Chorus 2
                     C
I wanna be   Bobby's girl,

             Am
I wanna be   Bobby's girl.

F   G   N.C.
That's the most important thing to me.

                C
And if I was   Bobby's girl,

        F   G   F   C
If I was   Bobby's girl, what a faithful, thankful girl ___ I'd be.

G   F   C N.C.
What a faithful, thankful girl ___ I'd be.

Outro
     N.C.   C
‖: I wanna be   Bobby's girl,

              Am
I wanna be   Bobby's girl. :‖ ***Repeat and fade***

EARLY ROCK   **31**

Calendar Girl

Words and Music by
Howard Greenfield and Neil Sedaka

Melody:

I love, I love, I love my cal-en-dar girl.

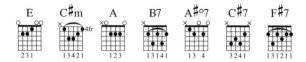

E   C#m   A   B7   A#°7   C#7   F#7

Intro

        E   **C#m**
        I love, I love, I love my calendar girl.

        E   **C#m**
        Yeah, sweet calendar girl.

        E   **C#m**
        I love, I love, I love my calendar girl

        A   **B7**   **E**
        Each and ev'ry day of the year.

Verse 1

            E
        (January.) You start the year off fine.

        C#m
        (February.) You're my little valentine.

            E
        (March.) I'm gonna march you down the aisle.

        C#m
        (April.) You're the Easter bunny when you smile.

Chorus 1

   A   A#°7
Yeah, yeah, my heart's in a whirl.

   E   C#7
I love, I love, I love my little calendar girl

   F#7   B7   E
Ev'ry day, (Ev'ry day.) ev'ry day ___ (Ev'ry day.) of the year.

   A   E
(Ev'ry day of the year.)

Verse 2

   E
(May.) Maybe if I ask your dad and mom

   C#m
(June.) They'll let me take you to the junior prom.

   E
(Ju - ly.) Like a firecracker, I'm aglow.

   C#m
(August.) When you're on the beach you steal the show.

Chorus 2   *Repeat Chorus 1*

Interlude   *Repeat Verse 1 (Instrumental)*

Chorus 3   *Repeat Chorus 1*

Verse 3

   E
(Sep - tember.) I'll light the candles at your "Sweet sixteen."

   C#m
(Oc - tober.) Romeo and Juliet on Halloween.

   E
(No - vember.) I'll give thanks that you belong to me.

   C#m
(De - cember.) You're the present 'neath my Christmas tree.

Chorus 4   *Repeat Chorus 1*

Outro

      E   C#m
‖: I love, I love, I love my calendar girl.

   E   C#m
Yeah, sweet calendar girl. :‖ ***Repeat and fade***

Cathy's Clown

Words and Music by
Don Everly

Melody:

Don't want your love   an - y -

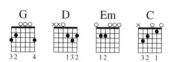

G	D	Em	C
32 4	1 3 2	1 2	32 1

Intro |G   D |G   D |G   D |G N.C. |

Chorus 1

                     G D G D   **G**   **D G**
Don't want your love ____ any - more.

    D   **G   D G D**   **G D G**
Don't want your kisses, ____ that's for sure.

    D   **Em**   **C**   **D N.C.**
I die each time I hear this ____ sound.

        G   **D G**   **D**   **G**   **D G N.C.**
Here he comes, ____ that's Cathy's clown.

Verse 1

                  G   **C G**
I've got to stand tall.

            C   **G**   **C G**
You know a man can't crawl.

             C   **Em**   **C**
For when he knows you tell lies and he lets 'em pass him by,

   D   **G C G N.C.**
He's not a man at all.

Chorus 2   *Repeat Chorus 1*

                                  G   C G

Verse 2   When you see me shed a tear

                     C   G   C G

        And you know that it's sincere,

                     C   Em   C

        Don't you think it's kind of sad that you're treating me so bad,

           D   G   C G N.C.

        Or don't you even care?

                          G D G D   G D G

Chorus 3   Don't want your love ____ any - more.

                 D   G   D G D   G D G

        Don't want your kisses, ____ that's for sure.

        D   Em   C   D N.C.

        I die each time I hear this ____ sound.

                 G   D G   D   G D

        Here he comes, ____ that's Cathy's clown.

               G   D   G   D

Outro   ‖: That's Cathy's clown. :‖ *Repeat and fade*

Come Go with Me

Words and Music by
C.E. Quick

Melody:

Dum, dum, dum, dum, dum - de doo-bie.

(Capo 1st fret)

G   Em7   Am7   D7   C   G7   C7

Intro

|:   G   Em7   Am7 D7
    Dum, dum, dum, dum, dum-de doobie.

G   Em7   Am7 D7
Dum, dum, dum, dum, dum, dum-de doobie.

G   Em7   Am7 D7
Dum, dum, dum, dum, dum, dum-de doobie.

G   C   G
Dum, wha, wha, wha, wha. :|

Verse 1

        G   Em7 Am7   D7
Well, love, love me, darlin',   come and go ___ with me.

G   Em7 Am7   D7
Please don't send me   way beyond ___ the sea.

G   Em7 Am7   D7   G Em7 Am7 D7
I need you, darlin',   so come go ___ with me.

Verse 2

        G   Em7   Am7   D7
Come, come, come, come,   come into ___ my heart,

G   Em7 Am7   D7
Tell me, darlin',   we will nev - er part.

G   Em7 Am7   D7   G C G G7
I need you, darlin',   so come go ___ with me.

Bridge 1

           C7
Yes, ___ I need you, yes, I really need you,

         G
Please ___ say you'll never leave me.

     C7
Well, ___ you say you never, yes, you really never,

     D7 N.C.
(You never give me a chance.)

Verse 3   *Repeat Verse 2*

Sax Solo

C7			G		
C7			D7 N.C.		
G Em7	Am7 D7	G Em7	Am7 D7	
G Em7	Am7 D7	G	G7	

Bridge 2   *Repeat Bridge 1*

Verse 4

G   **Em7 Am7**   **D7**
Love, love me, darlin',   come and go ___ with me.

G   **Em7**   **Am7**   **D7**
Please don't send me   way beyond ___ the sea.

G   **Em7 Am7**   **D7**   **G Em7**
I need you, darlin',   so come go ___ with me.

Outro

    Am7   **D7**   **G Em7**
‖: Come on ___ go with me.   :‖

Diana

Words and Music by
Paul Anka

Melody:

I'm so young and you're so old.

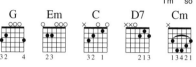

G   Em   C   D7   Cm

Intro

‖: G |Em |C |D7   :‖

Verse 1

G   Em
I'm so young and you're so old.

C   D7
This, my darling, I've been told.

G   Em
I don't care just what they say

C   D7
'Cause forever I will pray

G   Em
You and I will be as free

C   D7
As the birds up in the trees.

G   Em   C   D7   G Em C D7
Oh, please stay by me, Di - ana.

Verse 2

G   Em
Thrills I get when you   hold me close.

C   D7
Oh, my darling, you're the most.

G   Em
I love you but do you love me?

C   D7
Oh, Diana, can't you see

G   Em
I love you with all my heart

C   D7
And I hope we will never part.

G   Em   C   D7   G Em C D7
Oh, please stay with me, Di - ana.

Bridge

    C   **Cm**
Oh, my darling,   oh, my lover,

G
Tell me that there is no other.

C   **Cm**
I love you   with my heart.

N.C. (D7)
Oh, oh, oh, oh, oh, oh, oh, oh, oh, oh, oh, oh, oh.

Verse 3

G   **Em**
Only you can take my heart.

C   **D7**
Only you can tear it apart.

G   **Em**
When you hold me in your loving arms

C   **D7**
I can feel you giving all your charms.

G   **Em**
Hold me, darling, ho, ho, hold me tight.

  C   **D7**
A, squeeze me, baby, with, a, all your might.

G Em C   D7   G Em
Oh, please stay by me, Di - ana.

Outro

   C D7   **G   Em**
||: Oh, please, Di - ana.

C D7   **G   Em**
Oh, please, Di - ana.   :|| *Repeat and fade*

Dream Baby
(How Long Must I Dream)

Words and Music by Cindy Walker

Melody:

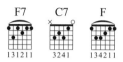

Sweet dream ___ ba - by.

F7   C7   F

131211 3241 134211

Intro |F7 | |

Chorus 1
C7
Sweet dream baby,

Sweet dream baby,

F7
Sweet dream baby,

C7   F
How long must I dream?

Verse 1
C7
    Dream baby, got me dreaming sweet dreams the whole day through.

    Dream baby, got me dreaming sweet dreams, the nighttime too.
F7
    I love you, and I'm dreamin' of you; that won't do.
C7
    Dream baby, make me stop my dreaming.
                                    F
    You can make my dreams come true.

Chorus 2   *Repeat Chorus 1*

Verse 2   *Repeat Verse 1*

Chorus 3   *Repeat Chorus 1*

Outro   *Repeat Chorus till fade*

El Paso

Words and Music by
Marty Robbins

Melody:

Out in the West Tex - as

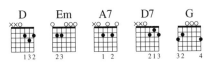

D   Em   A7   D7   G

Intro

```
|D        |        |Em      |        |
|A7       |        |        |D       |
|         |        |        |        |
```

Verse 1

          D   Em
Out in the West Texas town of El Paso,

A7   D
I fell in love with a Mexican girl.

                         Em
Nighttime would find me in Rosa's Cantina;

A7   D
Music would play and Felina would whirl.

                         Em
Blacker than night were the eyes of Felina,

A7   D
Wicked and evil while casting a spell.

                         Em
My love was deep for this Mexican maiden.

A7   D   D7
I was in love but in vain, I could tell.

G   D
One night a wild young cowboy came in, wild as the West Texas wind.

Dashing and daring, a drink he was sharing

                         G
With wicked Felina, the girl that I loved.

Verse 2

A7   D   Em
So, in anger I challenged his right for the love of this maiden.

A7   D
Down went his hand for the gun that he wore.

                        Em
My challenge was answered in less than a heartbeat;

  A7   D
The handsome, young stranger lay dead on the floor.

                  Em
Just for a moment I stood there in silence,

A7   D
Shocked by the foul, evil deed I had done.

                    Em
Many thoughts raced through my mind as I stood there.

A7   D   D7
I had but one chance and that was to run.

G   D
Out through the backdoor of Rosa's I ran, out where the horses were tied

I caught a good one, it looked like it could run.

                      G
Up on its back and away I did a ride.

Verse 3

A7   D   Em
Just as fast as I could from the West Texas town of El Paso,

A7   D
Out to the badlands of New Mexi - co.

               Em
Back in El Paso my life would be worthless.

A7   D
Ev'rything's gone in life, nothing is left.

               Em
It's been so long since I've seen the young maiden,

A7   D   D7
My love is stronger than my fear of death.

G   D
I saddled up and away I did go, riding alone in the dark.

Maybe tomorrow a bullet may find me;

                            G
Tonight nothing's worse than this pain in my heart.

Verse 4

       A7   **D**   **Em**
And at last, here I am on the hill over - looking El Paso.

A7   **D**
I can see Rosa's Cantina be - low.

                Em
My love is strong and it pushes me onward,

A7   **D**
Down off the hill to Felina I go.

              Em
Off to my right I see five mounted cowboys,

A7   **D**
Off to my left ride a dozen or more.

              Em
Shouting and shooting, I can't let them catch me.

A7   **D**   **D7**
I have to make it to Rosa's back door.

G   **D**
Something is dreadfully wrong, for I feel a deep burning pain in my side.

Though I am trying to stay in the saddle,

              G
I'm getting weary, unable to ride.

Verse 5

       A7   **D**   **Em**
But my love for Fe - lina is strong and I rise without falling.

A7   **D**
Though I am weary, I can't stop to rest.

              Em
I see the white puff of smoke from the rifle,

A7   **D**
I feel the bullet go deep in my chest.

              Em
From out of nowhere Fe - lina has found me,

A7   **D**
Kissing my cheek as she kneels by my side.

              Em
Cradled by two loving arms that I'll die for,

A7   **D**
One little kiss and, Felina, goodbye.

Eddie My Love

Words and Music by Aaron Collins,
Maxwell Davis and Saul Sam Ling

Melody:

Ed-die, my love, _____   I _____ love you so. _____

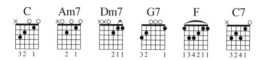

Intro

‖: C   Am7 | Dm7   G7   :‖

Verse 1

C   Am7 Dm7   G7
   Eddie, my love,   I love you so.

C   Am7   Dm7   G7
How I wanted for you,   you'll never know.

C   Am7 Dm7   G7   C Am7 Dm7 G7
Please, Eddie,   don't make me wait too long.

Verse 2

C   Am7 Dm7   G7
   Eddie, please write   me one line.

C   Am7   Dm7   G7
Tell me your love is   still only mine.

C   Am7 Dm7   G7   C F C C7
Please, Eddie,   don't make me wait too long.

Bridge 1

     F   **C**
You left me last Sep - tember

     F   **C**
To re - turn to me before long.

     F   **C**
But all I do is cry myself to sleep, Eddie,

              Dm7 G7
Since you've been gone.

Verse 3

  C   **Am7 Dm7**   **G7**
Eddie, my love,   I'm sinking fast.

  C   **Am7**   **Dm7**   **G7**
The very next day   might be my last.

  C   **Am7 Dm7**   **G7**   **C F C C7**
Please, Eddie,   don't make me wait too long.

Bridge 2   *Repeat Bridge 1*

Verse 4

  C   **Am7 Dm7**   **G7**
Eddie, my love,   I'm sinking fast.

  C   **Am7**   **Dm7**   **G7**
The very next day   might be my last.

  C   **Am7 Dm7**   **G7**   **C Am7 Dm7 G7**
Please, Eddie,   don't make me wait too long.

  C   **Am7 Dm7**   **N.C.**   **C**
Please, Eddie,   don't make me wait too long.

Fever

Words and Music by
John Davenport and Eddie Cooley

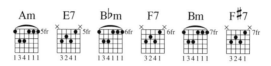

Intro   ‖: Am | |E7 |Am   :‖

Am

Verse 1   Never know how much I love you, never know how much I care.

                                  E7   **Am**
When you put your arms around me, I get a fever that's so hard to bear.

You give me fever when you kiss me, fever when you hold me tight,

       E7   **Am**
Fever in the morning, fever all through the night.

Am

Verse 2   Sun lights up the daytime, moon lights up the night.

                            E7   **Am**
I light up when you call my name, and you know I'm gonna treat you right.

You give me fever when you kiss me, fever when you hold me tight,

       E7   **Am**
Fever in the morning, fever all through the night.

Ev'rybody's got the fever, that is something you all know.

                    E7   **Am**
Fever isn't such a new thing, fever started long ago.

|B♭m | |F7 |B♭m |

Verse 3

B♭m
Romeo loved Juliet, Juliet, she felt the same.

                                          F7   B♭m
When he put his arms around her, he said, "Julie, baby, you're my flame.

Thou givest fever when we kisseth, fever with thy flaming youth.

           F7   B♭m
Fever, I'm afire, fever, yea, I burn for - sooth."

|Bm | |F♯7 |Bm |

Verse 4

Bm
Captain Smith and Pocahontas had a very mad affair.

                                          F♯7   Bm
When her daddy tried to kill him, she said, "Daddy, oh, don't you dare.

He give me fever with his kisses, fever when he holds me tight.

                    F♯7   Bm
Fever, I'm his missus. Oh, Daddy, won't you treat him right?"

Verse 5

Bm
Now you've listened to my story. Here's the point that I have made.

                                          F♯7   Bm
Chicks were born to give you fever, be it fah - renheit or centi - grade.

They give you fever when you kiss them, fever if you live you learn.

                    F♯7   Bm
Fever, till you sizzle, what a lovely way to burn.

F♯7   Bm
What a lovely way to burn.

F♯7   Bm
What a lovely way to burn.

F♯7   Bm   F♯7 Bm
What a lovely way to burn.

Galveston

Words and Music by
Jim Webb

Melody:

Gal - ves - ton, __ oh, Gal - ves - ton, _____

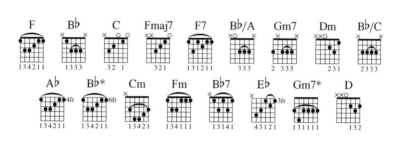

F   Bb   C   Fmaj7   F7   Bb/A   Gm7   Dm   Bb/C

Ab   Bb*   Cm   Fm   Bb7   Eb   Gm7*   D

Intro
```
|N.C.     |F        |         |         |
|    Bb  C|
```

Verse 1
```
F            Bb   C   F
```
Galveston, oh, Gal - ves - ton,

```
Fmaj7          F7          Bb    Bb/A Gm7
```
I still hear your sea - winds blow - ing.

```
C       F              Bb    Bb/A Gm7
```
I still see ____ her dark eyes glowing.

```
        C        Dm      Bb          Bb/C   F Bb C
```
She was twenty-one, ____ when I left Galveston.

Verse 2
```
F            Bb   C   F
```
Galveston, oh, Gal - ves - ton,

```
Fmaj7          F7          Bb    Bb/A Gm7
```
I still hear your sea - waves crashing.

```
C          F              Bb    Bb/A Gm7
```
While I watch ____ the cannons flashing,

```
        C        Dm      Bb          Bb/C   F Bb F
```
I clean my gun, ____ and dream of Galveston.

Bridge

A♭   B♭* A♭
I still see her standing by ____ the wa - ter,

Cm   A♭
Standing there looking out to sea.

    Fm   B♭7 E♭
And is she waiting there ____ for me,

    Gm7*   Fm B♭ C
On the beach ____ where we used to run?

Verse 3

F   B♭ C F
Galveston, oh, Gal - ves - ton,

Fmaj7   F7   B♭ B♭/A Gm7
I am so afraid ____ of dy - ing

  C   F   B♭ B♭/A Gm7
Be - fore I dry ____ the tears she's crying.

  C   Dm   C   B♭ B♭/A Gm7
Be - fore I watch ____ your sea birds fly - ing in ____ the sun

       D B♭/C   F
At Galveston, ____ at Galveston.

Outro   *Repeat Verse 1 (Instrumental) till fade*

Get a Job

Words and Music by Earl Beal,
Richard Lewis, Raymond Edwards
and William Horton

Melody:

Dip, dip, dip, dip, dip, dip,   dip.   Sha, na, na,   na,

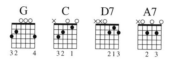

Intro

    N.C.
Dip, dip, dip, dip, dip, dip, dip.

Chorus 1

    G
  Sha, na, na, na, sha, na, na, na.

Ba, do, sha, na, na, na, sha, na, na, na.

    C
Ba, do, sha, na, na, na, sha, na, na, na.

    G
Ba, do, sha, na, na, na, sha, na, na, na.

    D7
Ba, yip, yip, yip, yip, yip, yip, yip, yip,

    C   G
Mum, mum, mum, mum, mum, mum. Get a job.

Sha, na, na, na, sha, na, na, na.

Verse 1

    G
Ev'ry mornin' about this time

She gets me out of my bed a cryin' get a job.

    C
After breakfast ev'ry day, she throws the want ads right my way

    D7   G
And never fails to say get a job.

Chorus 2

    Repeat Chorus 1

Bridge 1

        C   G

Well, when I get the paper, I read it through and through,

     A7   D7 N.C.

And ___ my girl never fails to say if there is any work for me.

Verse 2

N.C.

And then I go back to the house, hear that woman's mouth

Preachin' and a cryin' tell me that I'm lyin'

About a job that I never could find.

Chorus 3

N.C.

Sha, na, na, na, sha, na, na, na.

  G

Ba, do, sha, na, na, na, sha, na, na, na.

  C

Ba, do, sha, na, na, na, sha, na, na, na.

  G

Ba, do, sha, na, na, na, sha, na, na, na.

  D7

Ba, yip, yip, yip, yip, yip, yip, yip, yip,

  C   G

Mum, mum, mum, mum, mum, mum. Get a job.

Sha, na, na, na, sha, na, na, na.

Sax Solo   *Repeat Chorus 1 (Instrumental)*

Bridge 2   *Repeat Bridge 1*

Verse 3   *Repeat Verse 2*

Outro

  G

Sha, na, na, na, sha, na, na, na.

Ba, do, sha, na, na, na, sha, na, na, na.

  C

Ba, do, sha, na, na, na, sha, na, na, na.

  G

Ba, do, sha, na, na, na, sha, na, na, na.   *Fade out*

Good Golly Miss Molly

Words and Music by
Robert Blackwell and John Marascalco

Melody:

Good gol - ly Miss Mol - ly,

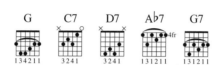

Intro

G			
C7		G	
D7	C7	G	N.C.

Chorus 1

　　　　　　　　　　　　G
Good golly, Miss Molly, sure likes to ball.

　　　　　　　　　　　C7　　　　　G
Good golly, Miss Mol - ly, sure likes to ball.

　　　　　　　　　　　　　　D7　　C7　　　　　　　　　G
When you're rockin' and rollin',　　can't hear your mama call.

Verse 1

　　　　　　　　　G N.C.　　　　　　　　　G N.C.
From the early, early mornin' to the early, early night,

　　　　　　　　　G N.C.
When I call Miss Molly rockin' at the House of Blue Light.

Chorus 2	**C7** **G**

C7   **G**

Chorus 2   Good golly, Miss Molly, sure likes to ball.

                            D7   **C7**   **G**

When you're rockin' and rollin',   can't hear your mama call.

                G N.C.   **G N.C.**

Verse 2   Mom and Papa told me, "Son, you better watch your step."

                G N.C.

If they knew about Miss Molly, have to watch my Pop myself.

Chorus 3   *Repeat Chorus 2*

Sax Solo   *Repeat Intro*

Chorus 4   *Repeat Chorus 1*

                G N.C.   **G N.C.**

Verse 3   I'm going to the corner, gonna buy a diamond ring.

                G N.C.

When she hugs me and kisses makes me ting-a-ling-a-ling.

                 C7   **G**

Chorus 5   Good golly, Miss Molly, sure likes to ball.

                          D7   **C7 N.C.**   **A♭7 G7**

When you're rockin' and rollin',   can't hear your mama call.

The Green Door

Words and Music by
Bob Davie and Marvin Moore

Mid - night, _   one more night _ with-out

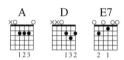

Intro | N.C. | A | | |

Verse 1
    A   D   A
Midnight, one more night without sleeping,

    D   A
Watching till the morning comes creeping.

    E7   A
Green door, what's that secret you're keeping?

Verse 2
             A   D   A
There's an old piano and they play it hot behind the green door.

             D
Don't know what they're doing but they laugh a lot

             A
Behind the green door.

          E7   D   A
Wish they'd let me in so I could find out what's behind the green door.

Verse 3

A   D   A
Knocked once, tried to tell him I'd been there.

D   N.C.   A
Door slammed,   hospitality's thin there.

E7   A
Wonder just what's goin' on in there.

Verse 4

A   D   A
Saw an eyeball peepin' through a smoky cloud behind the green door.

D
When I said "Joe sent me," someone laughed out loud

A
Behind the green door.

E7   D   A
All I wanna do is join the happy crowd behind the green door.

Piano Solo

A	D	A		
D		A		
E7	D	A		

Verse 5

A   D   A
Midnight, one more night without sleeping,

D   A
Watching till the morning comes creeping.

E7   A
Green door, what's that secret you're keeping?

E7   A
Green door, what's that secret you're keeping? Green door.

Greenfields

Words and Music by Terry Gilkyson,
Richard Dehr and Frank Miller

Once _ there were green fields   kissed by the sun.

(Capo 2nd fret)

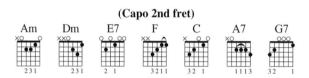

Intro |Am   Dm |Am   E7 |

Verse 1

Am   Dm   Am   E7
Once there were green fields   kissed by the sun.

Am   Dm   Am   E7
Once there were valleys where rivers used to run.

F   C   A7
Once there were blue skies with white clouds high a - bove.

Dm   G7   Am   E7
Once they were part of an everlasting love.

Am   Dm   Am   E7   F Am Dm E7
We were the lovers who strolled ___ through green fields.

Verse 2

Am   Dm   Am   E7
Green fields are gone now,   parched by the sun.

Am   Dm   Am   E7
Gone from the valleys where rivers used to run.

F   C   A7
Gone with the cold wind that swept into my heart.

Dm   G7   Am   E7
Gone with the lovers who let their dreams de - part.

Am   Dm   Am E7   F Am Dm E7
Where are the green fields that we ____ used to roam?

Bridge

F   C
  I'll never know what made you run a - way.

F   C
How can I keep searching when dark clouds hide the day?

Am   Dm
  I only know there's nothing here for me.

Am   Dm   E7
Nothing in this wide world left for me to see.

Verse 3

    Am   Dm   Am   E7
But I'll keep on waiting   till you re - turn.

Am   Dm   Am   E7
I'll keep on waiting un - til the day you learn

F   C   A7
You can't be happy while your heart's on the roam.

Dm   G7   Am   E7
You can't be happy un - til you bring it home.

Am   Dm   Am E7   Am Dm Am E7 Am
Home to the green fields and me ___ once a - gain.

Happy Birthday Sweet Sixteen

Words and Music by
Howard Greenfield and Neil Sedaka

Melody:

Tra, la, la, la, la, la, ___ la, la, la. Hap-py

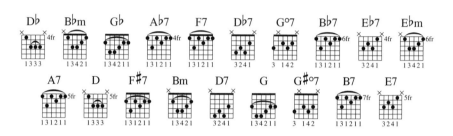

Intro

Db   Bbm
‖: Tra, la, la, la, la, la, ___ la, la, la.
Gb   Ab7
Happy birthday, sweet six - teen. :‖

Verse 1

Db   F7
Tonight's the night   I've waited for
Bbm   Db7
Because you're not a baby ___ anymore.
Gb   G°7   Db   Bb7
You've turned in - to the prettiest girl I've ever seen.
Eb7   Ab7
Happy birthday, sweet six - teen.

Verse 2

Db   F7
What happened to   that funny face?
Bbm   Db7
My little tomboy now wears ___ satins and lace.
Gb   G°7   Db   Bb7
I can't be - lieve my eyes, you're just a teenage dream.
Eb7   Ab7   Db
Happy birthday, sweet six - teen.

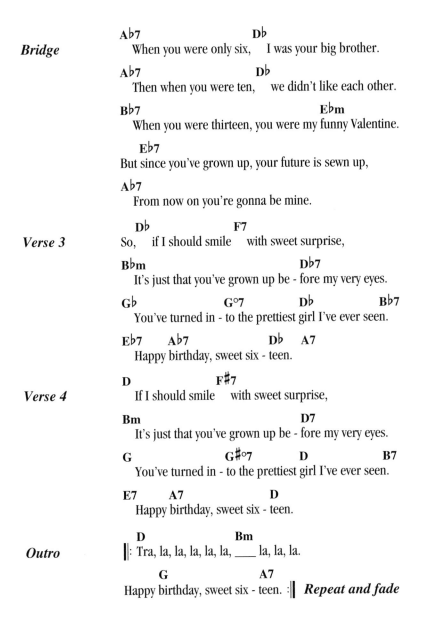

Bridge

A♭7   D♭
When you were only six,   I was your big brother.

A♭7   D♭
Then when you were ten,   we didn't like each other.

B♭7   E♭m
When you were thirteen, you were my funny Valentine.

E♭7
But since you've grown up, your future is sewn up,

A♭7
From now on you're gonna be mine.

Verse 3

D♭   F7
So,   if I should smile   with sweet surprise,

B♭m   D♭7
It's just that you've grown up be - fore my very eyes.

G♭   G°7   D♭   B♭7
You've turned in - to the prettiest girl I've ever seen.

E♭7   A♭7   D♭   A7
Happy birthday, sweet six - teen.

Verse 4

D   F♯7
If I should smile   with sweet surprise,

Bm   D7
It's just that you've grown up be - fore my very eyes.

G   G♯°7   D   B7
You've turned in - to the prettiest girl I've ever seen.

E7   A7   D
Happy birthday, sweet six - teen.

Outro

D   Bm
‖: Tra, la, la, la, la, la, ____ la, la, la.

G   A7
Happy birthday, sweet six - teen. :‖ *Repeat and fade*

Happy, Happy Birthday Baby

Words and Music by
Margo Sylvia and Gilbert Lopez

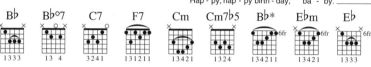

Verse 1

N.C.
Happy, happy birthday, baby.
Bb Bb°7 Bb

C7 F7 N.C.
Although you're with somebody new,

F7   Cm
Thought I'd drop a line to say

Cm7b5   Bb   Bb°7 Bb N.C.
That I wish this happy day would find me be - side you.

Verse 2

Bb Bb°7 Bb
Happy, happy birthday, baby.

C7 F7 N.C.
No, I can't call you my baby.

F7   Cm   Cm7b5
Seems like years ago we met on a day I can't for - get

Bb* Ebm Bb* N.C.
'Cause that's when we fell in love.

Bridge

Eb   Bb*
Do you re - member the names we had for ____ each other?

C7
I was your pretty, you were my baby.

F7 N.C.
How could we say goodbye?

Verse 3

Bb   Bb°7 Bb
Hope I didn't spoil your birthday.

C7 F7 N.C.
I'm not acting like a lady

F7   Cm   Cm7b5 N.C.
So I'll close this note to you with good luck and wishes too.

Bb
Happy, happy birthday, baby.

He's So Fine

Words and Music by
Ronald Mack

Doo, lang, doo,   lang, doo, lang. _

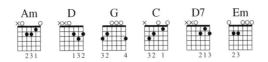

Intro

    Am   **D**
Doo, lang, doo, lang, doo, lang.

    Am   **D** **N.C.**
    Doo, lang, doo, lang.

Verse 1

          Am   **D**
He so fine. ____ (Doo, lang, doo, lang, doo, lang.)

               Am   **D**
Wish he were mine. ____ (Doo, lang, doo, lang, doo, lang.)

            Am   **D**
That handsome boy over there. (Doo, lang, doo, lang, doo, lang.)

               Am   **D**
The one with the wav - y hair. (Doo, lang, doo, lang, doo, lang.)

                     G
I don't know how I'm gonna do it, (Doo, lang, doo, lang, doo, lang.)

But I'm gonna make him mine. (Doo, lang, doo, lang, doo, lang.)

Be the envy of all the girls, (Doo, lang, doo, lang, doo, lang.)

                           N.C.
It's just a matter of time. (Doo, lang, doo, lang.)

	Am **D**
Verse 2	He's a soft spoken guy, ___ (Doo, lang, doo, lang, doo, lang.)

Am   **D**
Also seems ___ kind of shy. (Doo, lang, doo, lang, doo, lang.)

        Am   **D**
Makes me won - der if I (Doo, lang, doo, lang, doo, lang.)

            Am   **D**
Should even give ___ him a try. (Doo, lang, doo, lang, doo, lang.)

                      G
But then again he can't shy, ___ (Doo, lang, doo, lang, doo, lang.)

He can't shy away forever. (Doo, lang, doo, lang, doo, lang.)

And I'm gonna make him mine (Doo, lang, doo, lang, doo, lang.)

                      N.C.
If it takes me forever. (Doo, lang, doo, lang.)

Bridge

C
He so fine. (Oh, yeah.)

Gotta be mine. (Oh, yeah.)

G
Sooner or later, (Oh, yeah.)

I hope it's not later. (Oh, yeah.)

  C
We got to get together, (Oh, yeah.)

The sooner the better. (Oh, yeah.)

D7 N.C.   D7 N.C.
I just can't wait, I just can't wait

D7 N.C. D7 N.C. D7 N.C.
To be held in his arms.

Verse 3

               Am   D
If I were a queen ____ (Doo, lang, doo, lang, doo, lang.)

                      Am   D
And he asked me to leave ____ my throne, (Doo, lang, doo, lang, doo, lang.)

            Am   D
I'd do anything ____ that he asked, (Doo, lang, doo, lang, doo, lang.)

              Am   D
Anything to make ____ him my own. (Doo, lang, doo, lang, doo, lang.)

Outro

            G   Em
Oh, he so fine. ____ (So fine.) So fine. ____ (So fine.)

           G   Em
‖: So fine. ____ (So fine.) Oh, yeah. ____ (So fine.) :‖ *Repeat and fade*

Heartaches by the Number

Words and Music by Harlan Howard

Heart - ache   num - ber...

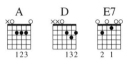

123   132   2 1

Verse 1

    A   **D**
Heartache number one was when you left me;

    E7   **A**
I never knew that I could hurt this way.

And heartache number two was when you

    D
    Came back again;

    E7   **A**
You came back and never meant to stay.

Chorus 1

    N.C.   **A**
Now, I've got heartaches by the number,

    D
Troubles by the score;

    E7
Ev'ry day you love me less,

                A
Each day I love you more.

    N.C.   **A**
Yes, I've got heartaches by the number,

    D
A love that I can't win,

      E7
But the day that I stop counting,

             A
That's the day my world will end.

Verse 2
         A   **D**
Heartache number three was when you called me,

    E7   **A**
And said that you were coming back to stay.

With hopeful heart I waited for your

D
  Knock on the door;

  E7   **A**
I waited, but you must have lost your way.

Chorus 2   ***Repeat Chorus 1***

I Can't Stop Loving You

Words and Music by Don Gibson

Melody:

Those hap-py hours...___

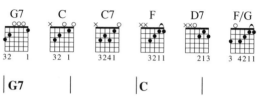

G7   C   C7   F   D7   F/G

Intro

|G7 | |C |

Verse 1

    G7   C   C7   F
Those happy hours___ that we once knew,

              C   D7 G7
Though long a-go, still make me blue.

           C   C7   F
They say that time___ heals a broken heart.

            C   G7   C F/G C
But time has stood still since we've been a-part.

Chorus 1

    C7   F
I can't stop loving you.

             C
So, I've made up my mind

    G7
To live in memory

          C   C7
Of old lonesome times.

      F
I can't stop wanting you;

      C
It's useless to say.

    G7
So, I'll just live my life

         C F/G C
In dreams of yester-day.

Verse 2   ***Repeat Verse 1***

              C7   **F**
Chorus 2   I can't stop loving you.

                      C
There's no use to try:

             G7
Pretend there's someone new,

           C   **C7**
I can't live a lie.

        F
I can't stop wanting you;

          C
The way that I do.

        G7
There's only been one love for me,

           C   **F**   **C**
That one love is you.

I Will Follow Him
(I Will Follow You)

English Words by Norman Gimbel
and Arthur Altman
French Words by Jacques Plante
Music by J.W. Stole and Del Roma

De, de,   do, de, de,   do,   de, de,   do, de, de, de, de,

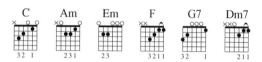

Intro

       C
(De, de, do, de de, do, de de, do, de, de, de, de,

Am
De, de, do, de de, do, de de, do, do, do, do, do.

C
Love him, I love him, I love him,

               Am   **N.C.**
And where he goes I'll follow, I'll follow, I'll follow.)

Verse 1

        C   **Em**
I will follow him, follow him wherev - er he may go.

     Am   **Em**
There isn't an ocean too ___ deep,

  F   **G7**   **C**   **Am N.C.**
A mountain so high it can ___ keep me a - way.

Verse 2

        C   **Em**
I must follow him. Ever since he touched my hand I knew

   Am   **Em**
That near him I always must be,

  F   **G7**   **C**
And nothing can keep him from me, he is my destiny.

Chorus 1

      C
I love him, I love him, I love him

               Am
And where he goes I'll follow, I'll follow, I'll follow.

                  C
He'll always be my true love, my true love, my true love,

                 Am   **N.C.**
From now until for - ever, forever, forever.

Verse 3

            C   **Em**
I will follow him, follow him wherev - er he may go.

      Am   **Em**
There isn't an ocean too deep,

      F   **Dm7 G7**   **C**   **N.C.**
A mountain so high it can keep, keep me a - way,

                 C   **N.C.**
Away from my love. (I love ya, I love ya, I love ya.)

Chorus 2   *Repeat Chorus 1*

Verse 4

            C   **Em**
I will follow him, follow him wherev - er he may go.

      Am   **Em**
There isn't an ocean too deep,

      F   **Dm7 G7**   **C**   **N.C.**
A mountain so high it can keep, keep me a - way,

                 C
Away from my love.

Outro

               Am
And where he goes I'll follow, I'll follow, I'll follow.

            C
‖: I know I'll always love ya, I love ya, I love ya.

               Am
And where he goes I'll follow, I'll follow, I'll follow. :‖ *Repeat and fade*

I'm Sorry

Words and Music by
Ronnie Self and Dub Albritten

Melody:

I'm sor-ry,   so sor - ry,

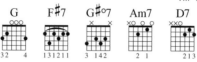

G   F#7   G#°7   Am7   D7

Intro |G |F#7 |G   G#°7 |Am7 D7 |

Verse 1
  G   F#7   G   G#°7
  I'm sorry, so sorry, that I was such a fool.
  Am7   D7 Am7   D7 G
  I didn't know ___ love could be so cruel.
  G#°7   Am7   D7
  Oh, oh, oh, oh, oh, oh, ___ oh, yeah.

Verse 2
  G   F#7   G   G#°7
  You tell me mistakes are part of being young,
   Am7   D7 Am7 D7   G G#°7 Am7 D7
  But that don't right the wrong that's been ___ done.

Verse 3
  G   F#7
  (I'm sorry.) *Spoken: I'm sorry.* (So sorry.) *So sorry.*
  G   G#°7
  Please accept my apol - ogy,
  Am7 D7   Am7   D7 G
  But love is blind and I was too blind to see.
  G#°7   Am7   D7
  Oh, oh, oh, oh, oh, oh, ___ oh, yeah.

Verse 4
  G   F#7   G   G#°7
  You tell me mistakes are part of being young,
   Am7   D7 Am7 D7   G
  But, that don't right the wrong that's been done.
  G#°7   Am7   D7
  Oh, oh, oh, oh, oh, oh, ___ oh, yes.

Verse 5
  G   F#7   G   G#°7
  I'm sorry, so sorry, please accept my apolo - gy,
   Am7   D7   Am7   D7 N.C.   G
  But love was blind and I was too blind to see. (Sorry.)

Itsy Bitsy Teenie Weenie Yellow Polkadot Bikini

Words and Music by
Paul Vance and Lee Pockriss

Melody:

She was a - fraid to come out of the

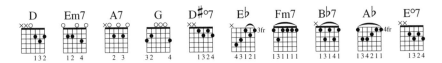

Intro

N.C.
(Bup, bup, bup, bup, da, bup, bup, bup, bup, bup.)

Verse 1

               D   Em7   A7
She was a - fraid to come out of the locker,

            Em7   A7   D
She was as nervous as she could be.

                               G
She was afraid to come out of the locker,

            D   Em7 A7   D N.C.
She was a - fraid that some - body would see.

(Two, three, four, tell the people what she wore.)

Chorus 1

A7 Em7 D#°7 A7   D
It   was   an   itsy, bitsy, teeny, weenie, yellow polka dot bikini,

A7   D
That she wore for the first time today.

A7   D
An itsy, bitsy, teeny, weenie, yellow polka dot bikini,

A7   G   D N.C.
So in the locker she wanted to stay.

(Two, three, four, stick around, we'll tell you more.)

(Bup, bup, bup, bup, da, bup, bup, bup, bup, bup.)

Verse 2

           D   **Em7 A7**
She was a - fraid to come out in the open,

        Em7   **A7**   **D**
And so a blanket a - round her she wore.

                        G
She was afraid to come out in the open,

          D   **Em7** **A7**   **D N.C.**
And so she sat bundled up on ___ the shore.

(Two, three, four, tell the people what she wore.)

Chorus 2

A7 Em7 D#°7 A7   **D**
It was an   itsy, bitsy, teeny, weenie, yellow polka dot bikini,

A7   **D**
That she wore for the first time today.

  A7   **D**
An itsy, bitsy, teeny, weenie, yellow polka dot bikini,

A7   **G**   **D N.C.**
So in the blanket she wanted to stay.

(Two, three, four, stick around, we'll tell you more.)

(Bup, bup, bup, bup, da, bup, bup, bup, bup, bup.)

GUITAR CHORD SONGBOOK

Verse 3

            E♭   Fm7 B♭7
Now she's a - fraid to come out of the water,

  Fm7   B♭7   E♭
And I wonder what she's gonna do.

                        A♭
Now she's afraid to come out of the water,

    E♭   Fm7 B♭7   E♭ N.C.
And the poor little girl's turnin' blue.

(Two, three, four, tell the people what she wore.)

Chorus 3

  B♭7 Fm7 E°7 B♭7   E♭
It   was an   itsy, bitsy, teeny, weenie, yellow polka dot bikini,

  B♭7   E♭
That she wore for the first time today.

  B♭7   E♭
An itsy, bitsy, teeny, weenie, yellow polka dot bikini,

  B♭7   A♭   E♭ B♭7 N.C.
So in the water she want - ed to stay.

Outro

  E♭   B♭7   E♭
(From the locker to the blanket, from the blanket to the shore.)

                 B♭7   E♭
(From the shore to the water.) Guess there isn't any more.

In the Still of the Nite

(I'll Remember)

Words and Music by
Fred Parris

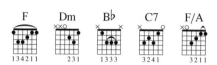

Intro

    F   **Dm**
(Shoo, doo, shoo, be, doo.   Shoo, doo, shoo, be, doo.

B♭   **C7**
Shoo, doo, shoo, be, doo.   Shoo, doo, shoo, be, whoa.)

Verse 1

            F   **Dm**   **B♭**   **C7**
In the still of the night, I held you, held you tight.

            F   **Dm**   **B♭**   **C7**
'Cause I love, love you so, promise I'll never let you go,

            F   **B♭**   **F/A**
In the still of the night. (In the still of the night.)

Bridge

            B♭   **F**
I re - member that night in May, the stars were bright above.

            B♭   **C7**
I'll hope and I'll pray to keep your precious love.

Verse 2

            F   **Dm**   **B♭**   **C7**
Well, be - fore the light, hold me a - gain, with all of your might,

            F   **B♭**   **F** **C7**
In the still of the night. (In the still of the night.)

Sax Solo   ‖: F | Dm | B♭ | C7   :‖
                   | F   B♭ | C7 |

Verse 3

                  F   Dm   B♭   C7
So, be - fore the light, hold me a - gain, with all of your might,

                  F   B♭   C7 N.C.
In the still of the night. (In the still of the night.)

In the still of the night.

Outro

        F   Dm
‖: (Shoo, doo, shoo, be, doo.   Shoo, doo, shoo, be, doo.

B♭
Shoo, doo, shoo, be, doo.

C7
Shoo, doo, shoo, be, do.) :‖ *Repeat and fade*

It's Only Make Believe

Words and Music by
Conway Twitty and Jack Nance

Melody:

Peo-ple see us   ev-'ry-where,   they think you _

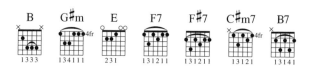

B   G#m   E   F7   F#7   C#m7   B7
1333 134111 231 13121 1 13121 1 13121 13141

Intro

|B   G#m|
People see us ev'rywhere,   they think you really care,

|E   F7|
But myself I can't deceive,

|F#7   B C#m7 F#7|
I know it's only make be - lieve.

Verse 1

|B   G#m|
My one and only prayer,   is that someday you'll care,

|E   F#7|
My hopes, my dreams come true,   my one and only you.

|E   F#7|
No one will ever know,   how much I love you so.

|B   B7   E|
My only prayer will be,   someday you'll care for me,

|F#7   E   B E B F#7|
But it's only make ___ be - lieve.

Verse 2

    B   **G♯m**
My hopes, my dreams come true,   my life I'd give for you.

    E   **F♯7**
My heart a wedding ring,   my all, my everything.

    E   **F♯7**
My heart I can't control,   you rule my very soul.

B7   **E**
My only prayer will be,   someday you'll care for me,

    F♯7   **E**   **B E B F♯7**
But it's only make ___ be - lieve.

Verse 3

    B   **G♯m**
My one and only prayer,   is that someday you'll care,

    E   **F♯7**
My hopes, my dreams come true,   my one and only you.

    E   **F♯7**
No one will ever know,   how much I love you so.

B7   **E**
My prayers, my hopes, my schemes,   you are my every dream,

    F♯7   **E**   **B**   **E**   **B E B**
But it's only make ___ be - lieve. (Make be - lieve.)

Johnny Angel

Words by Lynn Duddy
Music by Lee Pockriss

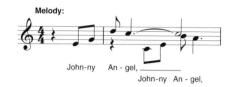

John-ny An - gel,
John-ny An - gel,

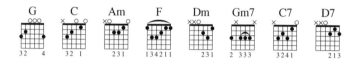

G   C   Am   F   Dm   Gm7   C7   D7

Intro

N.C.   G
Johnny Angel, Johnny Angel, Johnny Angel, Johnny Angel,
                          C
You're an angel to me.

Verse 1

                    C   Am
Johnny Angel, how I love him.

              F   Dm
He's got something that I can't re - sist.

              F   Dm G   C Am C Am N.C.
But he doesn't even know that I _____ e - xist.

Verse 2

                    C   Am
Johnny Angel, how I want him.

              F   Dm
How I tingle when he passes by.

              F   Dm   G   C Am C N.C.
Ev'ry - time he says, "Hello," my heart be - gins to fly.

Bridge 1
      Gm7   C7   Gm7   C7
I'm in heaven, ___ I get carried a - way.

  F N.C.   F N.C.
I dream of him and me and how it's gonna be.

      Am   D7   Am   D7   G N.C.
Other fellas ___ call me out for a date but I just sit and wait.

  F G N.C.
I'd rather concentrate on

Verse 3
        C   Am
Johnny Angel 'cause I love him,

      F   Dm
And I pray that someday he'll love me.

       F   Dm   G   C Am C N.C.
And to - gether we will see how lovely ___ heaven will be.

Bridge 2
      Gm7   C7   Gm7   C7
I'm in heaven, ___ I get carried a - way.

  F N.C.   F N.C.
I dream of him and me and how it's gonna be.

      Am   D7   Am   D7   G N.C.
Other fellas ___ call me out for a date but I just sit and wait.

I'd rather concentrate on

Verse 4
        C   Am
Johnny Angel 'cause I love him,

      F   Dm
And I pray that someday he'll love me.

       F   Dm   G   C
And to - gether we will see how lovely ___ heaven will be.

            Am   F   G   C
(Johnny Angel,   Johnny Angel.) Johnny Angel,   you're an angel to me.

Outro
            Am
‖: (Johnny Angel,   Johnny Angel.)

      F   G   C
Johnny Angel,   you're an angel to me. :‖ ***Repeat and fade***

Let It Be Me
(Je T'appartiens)

English Words by Mann Curtis
French Words by Pierre DeLanoe
Music by Gilbert Becaud

Melody:

I bless the day I found you,

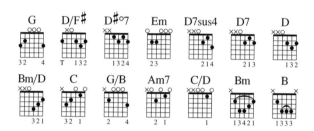

G   D/F♯   D♯°7   Em   D7sus4   D7   D
Bm/D   C   G/B   Am7   C/D   Bm   B

Intro | G | D/F♯ D♯°7 | Em | D7sus4 D7 |

Verse 1
G   D
I bless the day I found you,

Em   Bm/D
I want to stay around you,

C   G/B   Am7   C/D   G
And so I beg you,   let it ___ be me.

Verse 2
G   D
Don't take this heaven from one,

Em   Bm/D
If you must cling to someone,

C   G/B Am7   C/D   G
Now and for - ever,   let it ___ be me.

Bridge 1	C **Bm** **C** **G**

Bridge 1

     C   **Bm**   **C**   **G**
     Each time we meet love,   I find com - plete love.

     Am7   **G/B**   **C**   **B**
     Without your sweet love,   what would life be?

Verse 3

     G   **D/F#**
     So never leave me lone - ly,

     Em   **Bm/D**
     Tell me you'll love me only,

     C   **G/B** **Am7** **C/D**   **G**
     And that you'll always   let it ___ be me.

Bridge 2

     Repeat Bridge 1

Verse 4

     G   **D/F#**
     So never leave me lone - ly,

     Em   **Bm/D**
     Tell me you'll love me only,

     C   **G/B** **Am7** **C/D**   **G**
     And that you'll always ___   let it be me.

Let the Good Times Roll

Words and Music by
Leonard Lee and Shirley Goodman

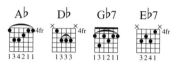

Come on, ba - by, let the good times _ roll. _____

Intro A♭ | D♭   A♭ | D♭   A♭ |

Verse 1
              D♭   A♭ D♭   A♭ D♭
Male: Come on, baby, let the good times roll.

          A♭ D♭   A♭
Come on, baby, let me thrill your soul.

G♭7   D♭
Come on, baby, let the good times roll,

E♭7   A♭
Roll all night long.

Verse 2
              D♭   A♭ D♭   A♭ D♭
Male: Come on, baby, yes, this is thick,

           A♭ D♭   A♭
This is something I   just can't miss.

G♭7   D♭
Come on, baby, let the good times roll,

A♭   D♭
Roll all night long.

Verse 3
            A♭ D♭   A♭   D♭   A♭ D♭
Female: Come on, baby, while the thrill is on.

          A♭ D♭   A♭
Come on, baby, lets have some fun.

G♭7   D♭
Come on, baby, let the good times roll,

E♭7   A♭
Roll all night long.

| | Db   Ab Db   Ab Db |
| *Verse 4* | *Female:* Come on, baby, just close the door. |

Ab Db   Ab
Come on, baby, let's rock some more.

Gb7   Db
Come on, baby, let the good times roll,

Ab   Db
Roll all night long.

| | Gb7 N.C.   Db N.C. Ab   Db N.C. |
| *Bridge 1* | *Female:* Feels so good   when you're home. |

Gb7 N.C.   Db N.C. Eb7 N.C.   Ab
Male: Come on, baby,   rock me all night long.

| | Db   Ab   Db   Ab Db |
| *Verse 5* | *Male:* Come on, baby, let the good times roll. |

Ab   Db   Ab
Come on, baby, let me thrill your soul.

Gb7   Db
Come on, baby, let the good times roll,

Ab   Db
Roll all night long.

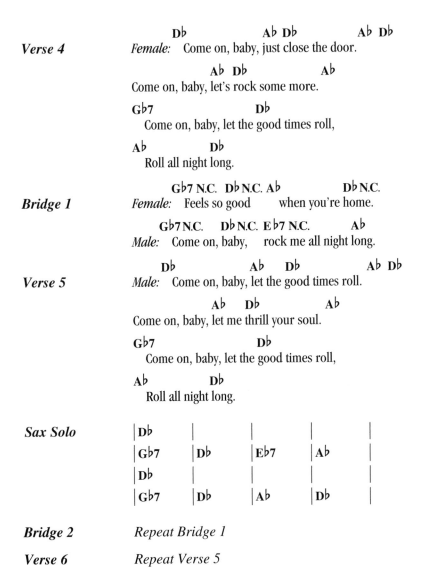

| *Sax Solo* | | Db | | | | | | | | |

| Bridge 2 | *Repeat Bridge 1* |
| Verse 6 | *Repeat Verse 5* |

Let's Twist Again

Words by Kal Mann
Music by Dave Appell and Kal Mann

Come on, __ let's twist a - gain, _

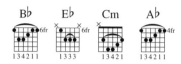

Intro

N.C.
Spoken: Come on, ev'rybody, clap your hands.

Awe, you lookin' good.

I'm gonna sing my song. It won't take long.

We're gonna do the twist and it goes like this.

Verse 1

Bb   Eb   Cm
Come on, let's twist again, like we did last summer.

Ab   Bb
Yeah, let's twist again, like we did last year.

Eb   Cm
Do you re - member when things were really hummin'?

Ab   Bb   Eb
Yeah, let's twist again,   twistin' time is here.

Bridge 1

Ab   Eb
Ee, a - round, 'n 'round' 'n up 'n down we go ___ again.

Ab   Bb
Oh, baby, make me know you love me so.

	E♭ Cm
Verse 2	Yeah, twist again, like we did last summer.

A♭   B♭   E♭   N.C.
Come on, let's twist again   like we did last year. *Twist.*

Sax Solo | E♭ | | Cm | |

| A♭ | | B♭ | N.C. |

E♭
Verse 3   *Who's that flyin' up there?*

Cm   A♭
Is it a bird? (No!) Is it a plane? (No!)

B♭   E♭
Is it the twister? ___ (Yeah!)

E♭   Cm
Verse 4   Yeah, twist again, like we did last summer.

A♭   B♭
Come on, let's twist again, like we did last year.

E♭   Cm
Do you re - member when things were really hummin'?

A♭   B♭   E♭
Come on, let's twist again,   twistin' time is here.

Bridge 2   *Repeat Bridge 1*

E♭   Cm
Verse 5   Then, come on, twist again, like we did last summer.

A♭   B♭   E♭
Girl, let's twist again,   like we did last year.

A♭   B♭   E♭
Come on, let's twist again,   twistin' time is here.

Little Darlin'

Words and Music by
Maurice Williams

Melody:

Lit - tle dar - lin',

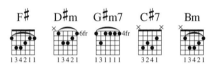

F# D#m G#m7 C#7 Bm

Intro

        F#   D#m   G#m7   C#7
(Ah, ya, ya, ya, ya, ya, ya, ya, ya, ya, ya, ya.)

Verse 1

         F#   D#m
Little darlin', oh, little darlin',

        G#m7   C#7
Oh, ho, ho, where a, are you?

        F#   D#m
My a, love, ah, I was wrong, ah,

        G#m7   C#7
To, oo, try to, oo, love two.

Ah, oo, ah, oo, ah, oo, ah,

        F#   D#m
Know well, ah, that my love ah,

        G#m7 C#7   F# Bm F#
Was just for you, ah, only you.

Verse 2

F#   D#m
Spoken: My darlin', I need ___ you

G#m7   C#7
To call my own and never do wrong.

F#   D#m
To hold in mine your little hand.

G#m7   C#7
I know too soon that all is so grand.

F#   Bm   F#
Please,   hold my hand.

Verse 3

F#   D#m
My dear, ah, a, I was wrong, ah,

G#m7   C#7
To, oo, try to, oo, love two.

Ah, oo, ah, oo, ah, oo, ah,

F#   D#m
Know, well, ah, that my love, ah,

G#m7 C#7   F# Bm F#
Was just for you, oh, only you.

Lollipop

Words and Music by
Beverly Ross and Julius Dixon

Lol - li - pop, lol - li - pop, oh, ___ lol - li, lol - li, lol - li,

G   Em   Am7   D7   C   G/D

Intro

N.C.
Lollipop, Lollipop, oh, lolli, lolli, lolli,

Lollipop, Lollipop, oh, lolli, lolli, lolli,

Lollipop, Lollipop, oh, lolli, lolli, lolli, Lollipop.

Ba, boom, boom, boom.

Chorus 1

G　　　Em　　　Am7　　D7
Lollipop, Lollipop, oh, ___ lolli, lolli, lolli,

G　　　Em　　　Am7　　D7
Lollipop, Lollipop, oh, ___ lolli, lolli, lolli,

G　　　Em　　　Am7　　D7　　G N.C.
Lollipop, Lollipop, oh, ___ lolli, lolli, lolli, Lollipop.

Ba, boom, boom, boom.

Verse 1

G　　　　C　　　G　　　C
Call my baby Lollipop,　tell you why,

G　　　　　　　　C　　D7
　His kisses sweeter than apple pie.

G　　　C　　　　G　　　　C
　And when he does his shaky rockin' dance,

G/D N.C.　　　　　　G N.C.
Man, I haven't got a chance.

<table>
<tr><td>*Chorus 2*</td><td>

D7   G   Em   Am7   D7
I call him Lollipop, lollipop, oh, ___ lolli, lolli, lolli,

G   Em   Am7   D7
Lollipop, Lollipop, oh, ___ lolli, lolli, lolli,

G   Em   Am7   D7   G N.C.
Lollipop, Lollipop, oh, ___ lolli, lolli, lolli, Lollipop.

</td></tr>
</table>

C   G   C   G

Bridge   Sweeter than candy on a stick, huckleberry, cherry, or lime.

C   D7
If you had a choice, he'd be your pick, but Lollipop is mine.

Chorus 3   *Repeat Chorus 1*

Verse 2

G   C   G   C
Crazy way he thrills of me,   tell you why,

G   C   D7
   Just like the lightning from the sky.

G   C   G   C
   He loves to kiss me till I can't see straight,

G/D N.C.   G N.C.
Gee, my Lollipop is great.

Chorus 4

D7   G   Em   Am7   D7
I call him Lollipop, Lollipop, oh, ___ lolli, lolli, lolli,

G   Em   Am7   D7
Lollipop, Lollipop, oh, ___ lolli, lolli, lolli,

G   Em   Am7   D7   G N.C.
Lollipop, Lollipop, oh, ___ lolli, lolli, lolli, Lollipop.

Ba, boom, boom, boom.

Outro

N.C.
Lollipop, Lollipop, oh, lolli, lolli, lolli,

Lollipop, Lollipop, oh, lolli, lolli, lolli,

                                                              G
Lollipop, Lollipop, oh, lolli, lolli, lolli, Lollipop, a Lollipop.

Lonely Boy

Words and Music by
Paul Anka

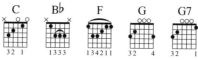

C	Bb	F	G	G7
3 2 1	1 3 3 3	1 3 4 2 1 1	3 2 4	3 2 1

Intro
| C Bb F C Bb F | C Bb F C |

Verse 1

       C   Bb F C   G   F G7
I'm just a lonely boy,   lonely and blue.

       G   F G   C Bb F C
I'm all a - lone   with nothing to do.

          Bb F C   G F G7
I've got ev'rything   you could think of,

       G   F G   C Bb F C N.C.
But all I want   is someone to love.

Chorus 1

                    C   G7
Someone, yes, someone to love, someone to kiss.

                      C
Someone to hold at a moment like this.

         G7
I'd like to hear somebody say,

                      C Bb F C Bb F C Bb F C
"I'll give you my love each night and day."

Verse 2   *Repeat Verse 1*

Chorus 2

                     C   G7
Somebody, somebody, somebody, please send her to me.

                      C
I'll make her happy, just wait and see.

                      G7
I prayed so hard to the heavens a - bove

                      C Bb F C Bb F C Bb F
That I might find someone to love.

Outro   *Repeat Verse 1 till fade*

(You've Got) The Magic Touch

Words and Music by
Buck Ram

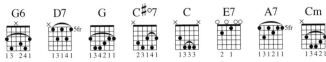

Verse 1

    N.C.   G6
You've got the magic touch.

        D7
It makes me glow so much.

                       G   C#°7 D7 N.C.
It casts a spell, it rings a bell, the magic touch.

Verse 2

            G6
Oh, when I feel your charm,

        D7
It's like a four alarm.

                                G   C G
You make me thrill so much, you've got the magic touch.

Bridge 1

            C   G
If I go reeling, oh, oh, I'm feeling the glow, oh, oh.

        E7   A7 D7 N.C.
But, where can I go from you?

Verse 3

        G6   D7
I didn't know too much, and then I felt your touch.

                                G   C G
And now I've learned I can return the magic touch.

Bridge 2   *Repeat Bridge 1*

Verse 4

        G6   D7
I didn't know too much, and then I felt your touch.

                          N.C.
And now I've learned I can return __ the magic touch.

            Cm   G
(Do, do, do, do, do, do, do, do, do.)

Lonely Teardrops

Words and Music by Berry Gordy,
Gwen Gordy Fuqua and Tyran Carlo

Melody:

My heart is cry-in', cry-in'.

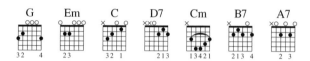

G   Em   C   D7   Cm   B7   A7

Intro

    G   Em
(Shoobie, do, ba, ba, ba.   Shoobie, do, ba, ba, ba.

    C   D7 N.C.
Shoobie, do, ba, ba, ba.)   My heart is cryin', cryin'.

Chorus 1

    C   Cm   G
Lonely tear drops,   my pillows never dry of   lonely teardrops.

                  D7   N.C.
Come home, come home.

Verse 1

                  G
Just say you will, say you will. (Say you will.)

           Em   C
Say you will. ___(Say you will.) Hey, hey.

          D7 N.C.
(Say you will.)   My heart is cryin', cryin'.

Chorus 2   *Repeat Chorus 1*

Verse 2	**G** Just say you will, say you will. (Say you will.)

          Em   **C**
Say you will. ___(Say you will.) Hey, hey.

          D7 N.C.
(Say you will.)

Bridge

        C   **Cm**
Just give me an - other chance for our ___ romance.

        G   **B7**
Come on, and tell me that one day you'll re - turn.

    C   **A7**
'Cause   everyday that   you been gone away

     D7 N.C.   **D7 N.C.**   **G N.C.**
You know my heart does nothing but burn. Cryin'.

Chorus 3   *Repeat Chorus 1*

Verse 3

          G
Just say you will, say you will. (Say you will.)

          Em   **G**
Say you will. ___(Say you will.) Hey, hey.

                              Em
(Say you will.) Say it right now, baby. (Say you will.)

                 G   **Em**
Come on, come on. ___ (Say you will.) Sing it louder you.

                         G
(Say you will.) Sing it right now, baby. (Say you will.)

                    Em
Yeah, come on, come on.   ***Fade out***

Lonesome Town

Words and Music by
Baker Knight

Melody:

There's a place where lov-ers   go __

Tune down 1/2 step:
(low to high) E♭ - A♭ - D♭ - G♭ - B♭ - E♭

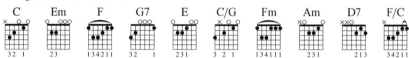

C   Em   F   G7   E   C/G   Fm   Am   D7   F/C

Intro

|C   Em |F   G7 |C   E |F   G7 |

Verse 1

C   C/G   E
There's a place where lovers go

F   G7   C   C/G
To cry their troubles a - way,

F   Fm   C   Am
And they call it   Lonesome Town,

F   G7   C
Where the broken hearts stay.

Verse 2

C   C/G   E
You can buy a dream or two

F   G7   C   C/G
To last you all through the years,

F   Fm   C   Am
And the only price you pay

F   G7   C   C/G
Is a heart full of tears.

Chorus

    F   Em
Goin' down to Lonesome Town,

    F   G7   C   C/G
Where the broken hearts stay.

    F   Em
Goin' down to Lonesome Town

    D7   G7
To cry my troubles a - way.

Verse 3

    C   C/G   E
In the town of broken dreams,

    F   G7   C   C/G
The streets are filled with re - gret.

    F   Fm   C   Am
Maybe down in Lonesome Town

    F   G7   C   C/G
I can learn to for - get.

    F   Fm   C   Am
Maybe down in Lonesome Town

    F   G7   C F/C C/G
I can learn to for - get.   (Lonesome Town.)

Lucille
(You Won't Do Your Daddy's Will)

Words and Music by
Richard Penniman and Albert Collins

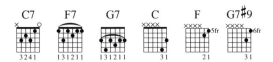

Lu - cille, ___   won't you do your sis-ter's

C7   F7   G7   C   F   G7#9

Intro

C7			
F7		C7	
G7	F7	C7	G7

Verse 1

          C7
Lu - cille, won't you do your sister's will?

          F7   C7
Lu - cille, won't you do your sister's will?

          G7
You ran off and left,

          F7   C7 N.C. (C) (F) (G7#9) (F)
But I love you still.

Verse 2

          C7
Lu - cille, please come back what you belong.

          F7   C7
Lu - cille, please come back what you belong. ___ Ooh, yeah.

          G7
I been good to you, baby,

F7   C7 N.C. (C) (F) (G7#9) (F)
Please, don't leave me alone.

GUITAR CHORD SONGBOOK

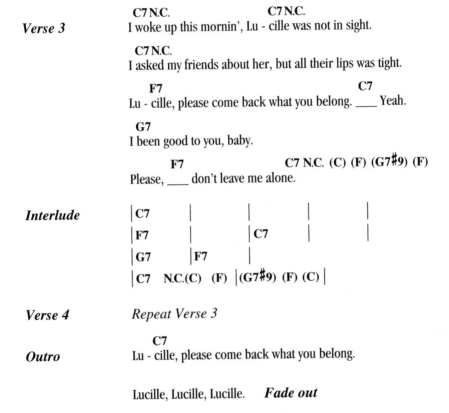

Verse 3

C7 N.C.   C7 N.C.
I woke up this mornin', Lu - cille was not in sight.

C7 N.C.
I asked my friends about her, but all their lips was tight.

  F7   C7
Lu - cille, please come back what you belong. ___ Yeah.

  G7
I been good to you, baby.

        F7   C7 N.C. (C) (F) (G7♯9) (F)
Please, ___ don't leave me alone.

Interlude

C7				
F7		C7		
G7	F7		
C7 N.C.(C) (F)	(G7♯9) (F) (C)

Verse 4

Repeat Verse 3

Outro

C7
Lu - cille, please come back what you belong.

Lucille, Lucille, Lucille.   ***Fade out***

Maybe Baby

By Norman Petty and
Charles Hardin

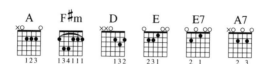

A   F#m   D   E   E7   A7

Intro

| A | F#m | A | F#m | |
| A | D E | A D | E | |

Verse 1

A   F#m
Maybe, baby, I'll ____ have you.

A   F#m
Maybe, baby, you'll ____ be true.

A   D   E   A   D E7
Maybe, baby, I'll ____ have you ____ for ____ me.

Verse 2

A   F#m
It's funny, honey, you ____ don't care.

A   F#m
You never listen to ____ my prayer.

A   D   E   A   D A
Maybe, baby, you ____ will love ____ me some - day.

GUITAR CHORD SONGBOOK

Bridge 1	**D** Well, you are the one that makes me glad,
	A **D** **A** And the other one that makes me sad.
	D **E** When someday you want me, well, I'll be there.
	Wait and see.
Verse 3	*Repeat Verse 1*
Verse 4	**A** **F♯m** Da, da, da, da, da, da, da, da, da, da, da, da, dum.
	A **F♯m** Da, da, da, da, da, da, da, da, da, da, da, da, dum.
	A **D** **E** Da, da, da, da, da, da, da, da, da, da, da, da, dum.
	A **D** **A** **A7** Oh, oh, oh.
Bridge 2	*Repeat Bridge 1*
Verse 5	**A** **F♯m** Maybe, baby, I'll ___ have you.
	A **F♯m** Maybe, baby, you'll ___ be true.
	A **D** **E** **A** **D** **E7** Maybe, baby, I'll ___ have you ___ for ___ me.
	A **D** **E** **A** **D** **A** Maybe, baby, I'll ___ have you ___ for ___ me. (You for me.)

Monster Mash

Words and Music by
Bobby Pickett and Leonard Capizzi

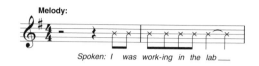

Spoken: I was work-ing in the lab ___

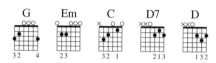

Verse 1

              G
Spoken: I was working in the lab late one night

      Em
When my eyes beheld an eerie sight,

      C
For my monster from his slab began to rise,

      D7
And suddenly, to my surprise...

Chorus 1

           G
(He did the Mash.) *He did the Monster Mash.*

           Em
(The Monster Mash.) *It was a graveyard smash.*

         C
(He did the Mash.) *It caught on in a flash.*

         D7
(He did the Mash.) *He did the Monster Mash.*

Verse 2

          G
From my laboratory in the castle east,

     Em
To the master bedroom where the vampires feast,

     C
The ghouls all came from their humble abodes

     D7
To get a jolt from my electrodes.

Chorus 2

          G
(They did the Mash.) *They did the Monster Mash.*

          Em
(The Monster Mash.) *It was a graveyard smash.*

          C
(They did the Mash.) *It caught on in a flash.*

          D7
(They did the Mash.) *They did the Monster Mash.*

Bridge

  C   **D**
The zombies were having fun. The party had just begun.

  C   **D N.C.**
The guests included Wolfman, Dracula and his son.

Verse 3

          G
The scene was rocking, all were digging the sounds.

Em
Igor on chains, backed by his baying hounds.

C
    The coffin bangers were about to arrive

    D7
With their vocal group: The Crypt-Kicker Five.

Chorus 3

          G
(They played the Mash.) *They played the Monster Mash.*

          Em
(The Monster Mash.) *It was a graveyard smash.*

          C
(They played the Mash.) *It caught on in a flash.*

          D7
(They played the Mash.) *They played the Monster Mash.*

Verse 4

G
Out from his coffin, Drac's voice did ring.

Em
Seems he was troubled by just one thing.

C
Opened the lid and shook his fist,

    D7 N.C.
And said,   *"What ever happened to my Transylvanian Twist?"*

Chorus 4

          G
(It's now the Mash.) *It's now the Monster Mash.*

          Em
(The Monster Mash.) *And it's a graveyard smash.*

          C
(It's now the Mash.) *It's caught on in a flash.*

          D7
(It's now the Mash.) *It's now the Monster Mash.*

Verse 5

      G
Now ev'rything's cool, Drac's a part of the band.

        Em
And my Monster Mash is the hit of the land.

      C
For you, the living, this mash was meant, too,

        D7 N.C.
When you get to my door, tell them Boris sent you.

Chorus 5

           G
(Then you can mash.) *Then you can Monster Mash.*

          Em
(The Monster Mash.) *And do my graveyard smash.*

          C
(Then you can mash.) *You'll catch on in a flash.*

          D7
(Then you can mash.) *Then you can Monster Mash.*

Outro

        G   **Em**
‖: (Wha-ooh, Monster Mash, wha-ooh, Monster Mash,

      C
Wha-ooh, Monster Mash,

      D7
Wha-ooh, Monster Mash.) :‖ *Repeat and fade w/*
                                      lead vocal ad lib.

Our Day Will Come

Words by Bob Hilliard
Music by Mort Garson

Melody:

Our day will __ come __

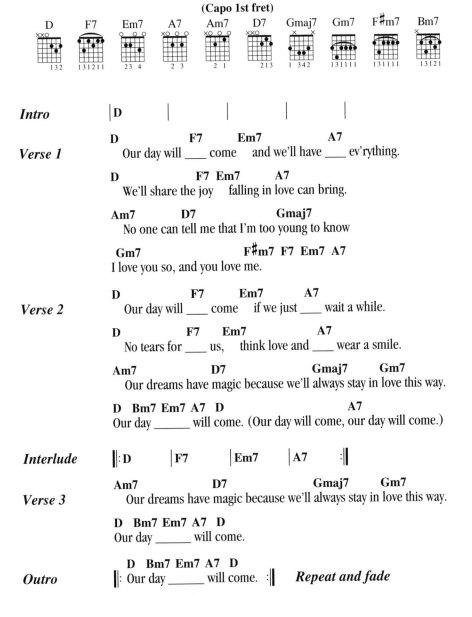

(Capo 1st fret)

D   F7   Em7   A7   Am7   D7   Gmaj7   Gm7   F#m7   Bm7

Intro |D | | | |

Verse 1

D   F7   Em7   A7
Our day will ___ come   and we'll have ___ ev'rything.

D   F7   Em7   A7
We'll share the joy   falling in love can bring.

Am7   D7   Gmaj7
No one can tell me that I'm too young to know

Gm7   F#m7 F7 Em7 A7
I love you so, and you love me.

Verse 2

D   F7   Em7   A7
Our day will ___ come   if we just ___ wait a while.

D   F7   Em7   A7
No tears for ___ us,   think love and ___ wear a smile.

Am7   D7   Gmaj7   Gm7
Our dreams have magic because we'll always stay in love this way.

D Bm7 Em7 A7 D   A7
Our day _____ will come. (Our day will come, our day will come.)

Interlude   ‖: D |F7 |Em7 |A7   :‖

Verse 3

Am7   D7   Gmaj7   Gm7
Our dreams have magic because we'll always stay in love this way.

D Bm7 Em7 A7 D
Our day _____ will come.

Outro   D Bm7 Em7 A7 D
‖: Our day _____ will come. :‖   ***Repeat and fade***

Mr. Lee

Words and Music by Heather Dixon,
Helen Gathers, Janice Pought,
Laura Webb and Emma Ruth Pought

Melody:

One, two, three, look at

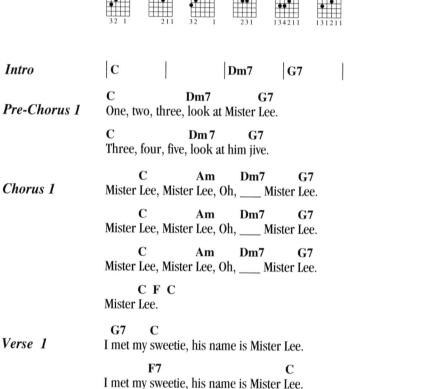

C   Dm7   G7   Am   F   F7

Intro |C | |Dm7 |G7 |

Pre-Chorus 1
     C   Dm7   G7
     One, two, three, look at Mister Lee.

     C   Dm 7   G7
     Three, four, five, look at him jive.

Chorus 1
         C   Am   Dm7   G7
     Mister Lee, Mister Lee, Oh, ___ Mister Lee.

         C   Am   Dm7   G7
     Mister Lee, Mister Lee, Oh, ___ Mister Lee.

         C   Am   Dm7   G7
     Mister Lee, Mister Lee, Oh, ___ Mister Lee.

        C F C
     Mister Lee.

Verse 1
     G7   C
     I met my sweetie, his name is Mister Lee.

     F7   C
     I met my sweetie, his name is Mister Lee.

                      Dm7   G7   C
     Well, he's the handsomest sweetie ___ that you ever did see.

               C
     My heart is achin' for you, Mister Lee.

     F7   C
     My heart is achin' for you, Mister Lee.

           Dm7 G7   C
     'Cause I love you so _____ and I'll never let you go.

Chorus 2	*Repeat Chorus 1*

Verse 2

<pre>
          G7   C
Here calls ___ Mister Lee, he's callin' for me.

           F7   C
Here calls Mister Lee, he's callin' for me.

          Dm7 G7   C
He's my lover boy, _____ let's jump for joy.

Come on, Mister Lee, and do your stuff.

              F7   C
Come on, Mister Lee, and do your stuff.

                   Dm7 G7   C
'Cause you're gonna be mine ___ till the end of time.
</pre>

Pre-Chorus 2   *Repeat Pre-Chorus 1*

Sax Solo

<pre>
‖:C   Am |Dm7 G7 :‖ Play 3 times
 |C   F |C   G7 |
</pre>

Pre-Chorus 3   *Repeat Pre-Chorus 1*

Chorus 3

<pre>
           C   Am   Dm7   G7
Mister Lee, Mister Lee, Oh, ___ Mister Lee.

           C   Am   Dm7   G7
Mister Lee, Mister Lee, Oh, ___ Mister Lee.

           C   Am   Dm7   G7
Mister Lee, Mister Lee, Oh, ___ Mister Lee.

           C F C G7
Mister Lee.
</pre>

Outro   *Repeat Chorus 3 till fade*

My Prayer

Music by Georges Boulanger
Lyric and Musical Adaptation by
Jimmy Kennedy

Melody:

When the twi-light is gone, —

(Capo 1st fret)

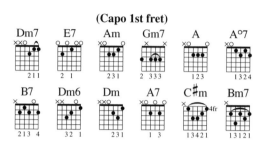

Dm7 E7 Am Gm7 A A°7

B7 Dm6 Dm A7 C#m Bm7

Intro

          N.C.   **Dm7 E7 N.C.**
          When the twilight is gone

                              Am N.C.
          And no songbirds are singing,

                              Dm7 E7 N.C.
          When the twilight is gone,

                              Am
          You come into my heart.

          Dm 7   Gm7   E7   A
          And here in my heart ___ you will stay ___ while I pray.

Verse 1

          A   A°7
          My prayer is to linger with you

          B7   Dm6 Dm   A   E7
          At the end of the day in a dream that's di - vine.

Verse 2

        A   A°7
My prayer is a rapture in blue

        B7   Dm6 E7   A Dm A A7
With the world far a - way   and your lips close to mine.

Bridge

      Dm   Am
To - night while our hearts are a - glow,

      Dm   B7   E7   N.C.
Oh, tell me the words   that I'm longing to know.

Verse 3

      A   A°7
My prayer and the answer you give,

         B7   Dm6
May they still ___ be the same.

           A C#m   Bm7 E7 N.C.
For as long as we live,   that you'll always be there.

          A Dm A Dm A N.C.
At the end of my prayer.

On Broadway

Words and Music by Barry Mann,
Cynthia Weil, Mike Stoller and Jerry Leiber

Melody:

They say the ne - on   lights   are bright

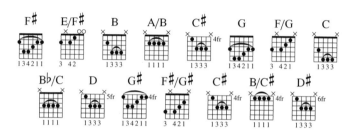

Intro   ‖: F♯ E/F♯ | F♯ E/F♯ :‖

Verse 1
    F♯   E/F♯ F♯ E/F♯
    They say the neon lights are bright

    F♯ E/F♯ F♯ E/F♯
    On Broad - way. (On Broad - way.)

    F♯   E/F♯ F♯ E/F♯ F♯ E/F♯ F♯ E/F♯ F♯
    They say there's always magic in the air. (On Broad - way.)

    B   A/B   B   A/B
    But when you're walking down that street

    B A/B B C♯
    And you ain't had e - nough to eat,

    F♯   E/F♯ F♯ E/F♯   F♯ E/F♯ F♯ E/F♯ F♯
    The glitter rubs right off and you're no - where. (On Broad - way.)

Verse 2
           G   F/G   G   F/G
           They say the girls are something else

           G   F/G   G   F/G
           On Broad - way. (On Broad - way.)

           G   F/G G F/G   G F/G   G   F/G G
           But looking at them just gives me the blues.   (On Broad - way.)

           C   B♭/C C   B♭/C
           'Cause how you gonna make some time

           C   B♭/C   C   D
           When all you got is one thin ___ dime?

           G   F/G   G   F/G   G F/G   G   F/G G
           And one thin dime won't even shine your shoes. (On Broad - way.)

Verse 3
           G♯   F♯/G♯ G♯   F♯/G♯
           They say that I won't last too long

           G♯   F♯/G♯   G♯   F♯/G♯
           On Broad - way. (On Broad - way.)

           G♯   F♯/G♯   G♯ F♯/G♯
           I'll catch a Greyhound bus for home,

                  G♯ F♯/G♯ G♯   F♯/G♯G♯
           They all ___ say.   (On Broad - way.)

              C♯   B/C♯   C♯   B/C♯
           But, oh, they're dead wrong, I know they are,

           C♯   B/C♯   C♯   D♯
            'Cause I can play this here gui - tar,

           G♯   F♯/G♯   G♯   F♯/G♯ G♯   F♯/G♯   G♯   F♯/G♯
           And I won't quit till I'm a star on Broad - way. (On Broad - way.)

Interlude   ‖: G♯ F♯/G♯ | G♯ F♯/G♯ | G♯ F♯/G♯ | G♯ F♯/G♯ :‖

Verse 4
              C♯   B/C♯   C♯   B/C♯
           But, oh, they're dead wrong, I know they are,

           C♯   B/C♯   C♯   D♯
            'Cause I can play this here gui - tar,

           G♯   F♯/G♯   G♯   F♯/G♯ G♯   F♯/G♯   G♯   F♯/G♯
           And I won't quit till I'm a star on Broad - way. (On Broad - way.)

Outro
              G♯   F♯/G♯ G♯   F♯/G♯
       ‖: On Broad - way. (On Broad - way.)   :‖   ***Repeat and fade***
                                                 w/ lead vocal ad lib.

Only the Lonely

(Know the Way I Feel)

Words and Music by
Roy Orbison and Joe Melson

Melody:

On-ly   the   lone-ly

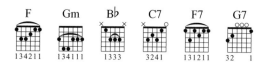

Intro

|N.C.| |F|
(Dum, dum, dum, dum-be, doo, wah.

Gm
Oh, yeah, yeah, yeah, yeah.

B♭   **C7**
Oh, whoa, oh, oh, oo-wah.

F   **C7**
Only the lonely.

F   **N.C.**
Only the lonely.)

Verse 1

F
Only the lonely

          Gm
Know the way I feel to-night.

C7
Only the lonely

          B♭   **F**
Know this feeling ain't right.

	N.C. F
Bridge	There goes my baby,

N.C.   **F7**
There goes my heart.

N.C.   **B♭**
They're gone forever;

N.C.   **G7**   **C7**
So far apart.

N.C.   **F**   **B♭**   **C7**
But only the lonely know why   I cried.

       F
Only the lonely.

Interlude	*Repeat Intro*

       F

Verse 2	Only the lonely

                        Gm
Know the heartaches I've been through.

C7
Only the lonely

      B♭   **F**
Know I cry and cry for you.

	N.C. F
Outro	Maybe to-morrow

N.C.   **F7**
A new romance,

N.C.   **B♭**
No more sorrow.

N.C.   **G7**   **C7**
But that's the chance

N.C.
You gotta take

      B♭   **C7**
If your lonely heart breaks.

       F
Only the lonely.

Party Doll

Words and Music by
James Bowen and Buddy Knox

Melody:

Well, all ___ I want _ is a

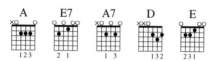

A   E7   A7   D   E

Verse 1

            A **E7**   **A**
Well, all ____ I want is a party doll.

                    E7   **A**
Come along with me, we're feelin' wild.

              E7 **A**
To be ever lovin' true and fair.

           N.C.
To run ____ her fingers a through my hair.

Chorus 1

           A
Come ____ along and be my party doll.

E7   **A**
Come along and be my par - ty doll.

            A7   **D**
Come along and be my par - ty doll.

      E   **A**
I'll ____ make love to you, to you.

      E   **A**
I'll ____ make love to you.

Verse 2

    A   E7   A
Well, I saw a gal a walkin' down the street,

                    E7   A
The kind of a gal ___ I'd love to meet.

            E7   A
She had blond hair and eyes of blue.

         N.C.
Baby, ___ I want to have a party with you.

Chorus 2   *Repeat Chorus 1*

Guitar Solo 1 |A N.C. |A N.C. |A N.C. |A7 N.C. |
                    |D | |A | |
                    |D | |E |A |

Bridge

    A   D   A
Ev'ry man has gotta have a party doll

    E7   A
To be with him a when he's feelin' wild,

                D
To be ever lovin', true and fair,

    E7   A
To run her fingers through his hair,

    E7   A
To run her fingers through his hair.

Chorus 3   *Repeat Chorus 1*

Guitar Solo 2   *Repeat Guitar Solo 1*

Chorus 4   *Repeat Chorus 1*

Outro   ‖: A   D |A   :‖ *Repeat and fade*
               Oo. _____

Peppermint Twist

Words and Music by
Joseph DiNicola and Henry Glover

Melody:

Well, got a new dance and it go like

G7   F7   C7

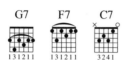

131211   131211   3241

Intro
| G7 | | | F7 | | |
| C7 | | | | | |

Verse 1
C7
Well, got a new dance and it go like this,

(Ba, shoo, ba, ba, ba, ba, ba, shoo, ba.)

F7
Yeah, the name of this dance is the peppermint twist.

C7
(Ba, shoo, ba, ba, ba, ba, ba, shoo, ba.)

G7   F7   C7
And you'll like ___ it like this, ___ peppermint twist.

(Ba, shoo, ba, ba, ba, ba, shoo, ba.)

Bridge
C7
Yeah, 'round and 'round, up and down,

F7   C7
'Round and 'round, up and down,

G7   F7
'Round and 'round and   up and down,

C7 N.C.
And one, two, three, kick. One, two, three, jump!

Guitar Solo	‖: C7				
	| F7		| C7		
	| G7	| F7	| C7		:‖

Verse 2

       C7
Well, meet me, baby, on forty-fifth street.

(Ba, shoo, ba, ba, ba, ba, ba, shoo, ba.)

F7
  Where the peppermint twisters meet.

C7
  (Ba, shoo, ba, ba, ba, ba, shoo, ba.)

          G7   **F7**   **C7**
And you learn ____ to do this, ____ peppermint twist.

(Ba, shoo, ba, ba, ba, ba, shoo, ba.)

Verse 3

       C7
It's all right, all night, it's all right.

(It's all right, it's all right, it's all right.)

   F7   **C7**
It's o - kay, all day, it's okay. ____ (It's okay, it's okay, it's okay.)

     G7   **F7**   **C7**
When you learn ____ to do this, ____ the peppermint twist.

(Ba, shoo, ba, ba, ba, ba, shoo, ba.)

Verse 4

   C7
Hey, yeah. (Hey, yeah.) Hey, yeah. (Hey, yeah.)

 F7   **C7**
Hey, yeah. (Hey, yeah.) Hey, yeah. (Hey, yeah.)

     G7   **F7**   **C7**
Hey, yeah, yeah. (Hey, yeah, yeah.) Hey, yeah, yeah. (Hey, yeah, yeah.)

Outro   *Repeat Verse 4 w/ vocal ad lib.*

Poor Little Fool

Words and Music by
Sharon Sheeley

Melody:

I used to play a - round _ with hearts _

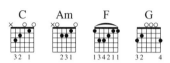

Intro

| | C | | Am | | F | | G | |
| | C | | Am | | F | | G | |

(Oo.) _____

Verse 1

C   Am   F   G
I used to play around ___ with hearts that hastened at my call,

C   Am   F   G
But when I met that little girl I knew that I would fall.

Chorus 1

C   Am
Poor little fool, ___ oh, yeah.

F   G   C
I was a fool, ___ uh huh.

Am   F   G
(Uh huh, poor little fool. I was a fool, oh, yeah.)

Verse 2

C   Am   F   G
She'd play around and tease ___ me with her care - free devil eyes.

C   Am   F   G
She'd hold me close and kiss ___ me, but her heart ___ was full of lies.

Chorus 2   *Repeat Chorus 1*

```
                 C                  Am             F                 G
```
Verse 3   She told me how she cared ___ for me and that we'd never part.

```
                 C             Am        F            G
```
And so for the very first ___ time, I gave away my heart.

Chorus 3   *Repeat Chorus 1*

```
                 C                  Am        F                 G
```
Verse 4   The next day she was gone ___ and I knew she lied to me.

```
                 C            Am          F            G
```
She left me with a bro - ken heart and won her victo - ry.

Chorus 4   *Repeat Chorus 1*

```
                      C                 Am            F                G
```
Verse 5   Well, I've played this game with oth - er hearts, but I never thought I'd see

```
                 C                   Am              F               G
```
The day when someone else ___ would play love's foolish game with me.

Chorus 5   *Repeat Chorus 1*

```
                          C      Am
```
Chorus 6   Poor little fool, ___ oh, yeah.

```
                 F          G        C
```
I was a fool, ___ uh huh.

```
                     F
```
(Uh huh, poor little fool.

```
                   C
```
Poor little fool. Poor little fool.)

Puppy Love

Words and Music by
Paul Anka

Melody:

And they called it pup-py love, _____

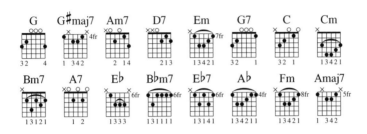

Intro

| G G#maj7 | G   N.C. |

Verse 1

                      Am7
And they called it puppy love,

D7   **G**
Oh, I guess they'll never know

Em   **Am7**
How a young heart   really feels

D7   **G G#maj7 G N.C.**
And why I love her so.

Verse 2

                    Am7
And they called it puppy love

D7   **G**
Just because we're, we're seventeen.

Em   **Am7**
Tell them all it, please tell them isn't fair

D7   **G**   **G#maj7 G G7**
To take away my only dream.

Bridge

```
        C              Cm            G              G7
I cry each night my tears for you, my tears are all in vain.
```

```
        C                    Bm7
I'll hope and I'll pray that ____ may, maybe someday
```

```
        A7                    D7
You'll be back in my arms once a - gain.
```

```
                              N.C.
(You'll be back in my arms once a - gain.)
```

Verse 3

```
                                    Am7
Someone help me, help me, help me please,
```

```
D7           G
  Is the answer    up above?
```

```
Em            Am7
  How can I, oh, ____ how can I tell them
```

```
D7              G                    Eb N.C.
  This is not a puppy love? (This is not a puppy love.)
```

Verse 4

```
                      Bbm7
Someone help me, help me, help me please,
```

```
Eb7           Ab
  Is the answer    up above?
```

```
Fm            Bbm7
  How can I ever ____ tell them
```

```
Eb7     N.C.          Ab  Amaj7 Ab
  This is not a puppy love?        (This is not a puppy love.)
```

Put Your Head on My Shoulder

Words and Music by
Paul Anka

Put your head on   my shoul - der,

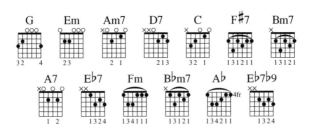

Intro | G   Em |Am7 D7 |G   C |G N.C. |

Verse 1

                              Em   Am7   D7
Put your head on my shoulder,   hold me in your arms,

G   Em Am7   D7
Ba - by.   Squeeze me, oh, so tight,

G   Em Am7   D7   G Em G N.C.
Show me   that you love me too.

Verse 2

                             Em   Am7   D7
Put your lips next to mine, dear.   Won't you kiss me once?

G   Em Am7 D7
Ba - by,   just a kiss goodnight,

G   Em Am7   D7   G   C   G
May - be   you and I will fall in love. (You and I will fall in love.)

Bridge
```
            D7        G            D7            G
People say that love's a game, a game you just can't win.

F#7          Bm7             A7              D7 N.C.
If there's a way I'll find it someday, and then this fool will rush in.
```

Verse 3
```
                    Em    Am7     D7
Put your head on my shoulder,    whisper in my ear,

G   Em Am7    D7
Ba - by,    words I want to hear.

G   Em Am7    D7          G
Tell me,    tell me that you love me too.

                    Eb7 N.C.
(Tell me that you love me too.)
```

Verse 4
```
                    Fm      Bbm7    Eb7
Put your head on my shoulder,    whisper in my ear,

Ab   Fm  Bbm7   Eb7
Ba - by,     words I want to hear.

Ab   Fm Bbm7    Eb7       Ab     Fm Bbm7 Eb7b9 Ab
Ba - by,    put your head on my shoulder.
```

Raindrops

Words and Music by
Dee Clark

Ah,   rain - drops,   so man-y

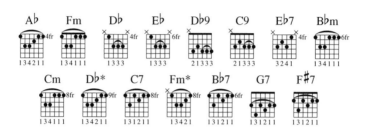

Intro | A♭ | | | |

Verse 1
      A♭ Fm D♭ E♭   A♭ Fm
Ah, rain - drops,   so many rain - drops,

     D♭ E♭   A♭ Fm D♭9 C9   Fm
It feels like rain - drops   fall - ing from my eyes,

           A♭
Falling from my eyes.

Verse 2
    E♭7   A♭   Fm D♭ E♭   A♭ Fm D♭
Since my love has left me   I'm ___ so all a - lone.

    E♭   A♭   Fm D♭9   C9   Fm
I would bring her ___ back to me   but I don't know where she's gone,

            A♭
I don't know where she's gone.

Bridge 1

Ab Bbm Cm Db*   Cm
There must be a cloud in my head,

Bbm   Ab
Rain keeps falling from my eyes.

C7   Fm*
Oh, no, it can't be teardrops

   Bb7   Eb Db Cm Bbm Eb N.C.
For a man ain't supposed to cry.

Verse 3

         Ab Fm Db Eb   Ab Fm
So it must be rain - drops,   so many rain - drops,

Db Eb   Ab Fm Db9 C9   Fm
It feels like rain - drops   fall - ing from my eyes,

      Ab N.C.
Falling from my eyes.

Interlude

| Ab Fm | Db Eb | Ab Fm | Db Eb |
| Ab Fm | Db9 C9 | Fm G7 | F#7 |
| Ab |

Bridge 2

Repeat Bridge 1

Verse 4

         Ab Fm Db Eb   Ab Fm
So it must be rain - drops,   so many rain - drops,

Db Eb   Ab Fm Db9 C9   Fm
It feels like rain - drops   fall - ing from my eyes,

      Ab
Falling from my eyes.

Outro

      Fm   Ab
‖: It keeps on fallin', fallin' from my eyes. :‖ *Repeat and fade w/ vocal ad lib.*

Rockin' Robin

Words and Music by
J. Thomas

Melody:

(Tweet - a - lee, deet - a - lee-dee,   tweet-a - lee, deet - a - lee-dee.)

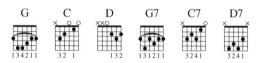

G   C   D   G7   C7   D7

Intro

N.C.(G)   (C)   (D)
(Tweetalee, deetaleedee,   tweetalee, deetaleedee.

(G)   (C)   (D)
Tweetalee, deetaleedee,   tweetalee, deetaleedee.

(G)   (C)   (D)
Tweetalee, deetaleedee,   tweetalee, deetaleedee,

(G)
Tweet, tweet, tweet, tweet.)

Verse 1

G7 N.C.
He rocks in the treetop all the day long,

G7 N.C.
Hop - pin' and a boppin' and a singin' his song.

G7 N.C.
All ___ the little birds on Jaybird Street

G7 N.C.
Love   to hear the robin go tweet, tweet, tweet.

Chorus 1

C7   G
Rockin' robin,   rock, rock, rockin' robin.
          (Tweet, tweet,   tweet.   Tweet, tweetaleedee.)

D7
Blow ___ rockin' robin

                              G
'Cause we're really gonna rock tonight.   Yeah.
                              (Tweet, tweet,   tweetaleedee.)

Verse 2   **G7 N.C.**
Ev - 'ry little swallow, ev'ry chickadee,

G7 N.C.
Ev - 'ry little bird in the tall oak tree.

G7 N.C.
The wise old owl, the big black crow,

G7 N.C.
Flap - pin' their wings, singin' go bird go.

Chorus 2   **C7**   **G**
Rockin' robin,   rock, rock, rockin' robin.
           (Tweet, tweet, tweet.   Tweet, tweetaleedee.)

D7
Blow ___ rockin' robin

                        G
'Cause we're really gonna rock tonight.   Blow!
            (Tweet, tweet, tweetaleedee.)

Piccolo Solo | **G** | | | **G7** |
            (Tweetla, deetladee, tweetaleedee, tweet,   tweetaleedee.

    | **C7** | | **G** | |
     Tweet, tweet,   tweetaleetweet, tweet,   tweetaleedee.

    | **D7** | **C7** | **G** | |
     Oo, oo, oo, oo,   oo, oo, oo, oo, tweet, tweet,   tweetaleedee.)

Bridge 1   **C7**
A pretty little raven at the bird band stand

           G
Taught ___ them how to do the bop and it was grand.

          C7
They started going steady and, bless my soul,

        D7 N.C.
He out bopped the buzzard and the oriole.

Verse 3	*Repeat Verse 1*

                C7   **G**

Chorus 3   Rockin' robin,   rock, rock, rockin' robin.

                    (Tweet, tweet,   tweet.   Tweet, tweetaleedee.)

          D7

Blow ____ rockin' robin

                          G

'Cause we're really gonna rock tonight.   Go rock!

                     (Tweet, tweet,   tweetaleedee.)

Bridge 2	*Repeat Bridge 1*
Verse 4	*Repeat Verse 1*

                C7   **G**

Chorus 4   Rockin' robin,   rock, rock, rockin' robin.

                    (Tweet, tweet,   tweet.   Tweet, tweetaleedee.)

             D7

Blow ____ rockin' robin

                          G

'Cause we're really gonna rock tonight.   Rock!

                     (Tweet, tweet,   tweetaleedee.)

              N.C.(G)   **(C)**   **(D)**

Outro   ‖: (Tweetalee, deetaleedee,   tweetalee, deetaleedee. :‖

       (G)   **(C)**   **(D)**   **(G)**

       Tweetalee, deetaleedee,   tweetalee, deetaleedee, tweet, tweet.)

Ruby Baby

Words and Music by
Jerry Leiber and Mike Stoller

Oh, ___ I said, I love a girl and, uh, ___

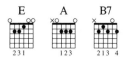

E A B7

Intro | E | |

                      E

Verse 1   Oh, I said, I love a girl and, uh, Ruby is her name.

                      Hear me talkin' now.

                      This, girl don't love me, but I love her just the same.

                      What I say?

                      A

Chorus 1   Whoa, ___ Ruby, Ruby, how I want ya.

               E

                      Like a ghost, I'm, uh, gonna haunt ya.

               B7   A   E

                      Ruby, Ruby, Ru - by will you be mine?

                      Ah, sometime.

	E
Verse 2	Ah, each time I see you, baby, my heart cries.
	Ah, it does, Ruby.
	I tell ya, I'm gonna steal you alway from all those guys.
	Idea was,
	A
Chorus 2	Whoa, ____ from the happy day I met ya, now,
	E
	I made a bet that I was going to get ya.
	B7 **A** **E**
	Now, Ruby, Ruby, Ruby will you be mine?
	Hear me talkin'. In time now. Hip, now.
	E
Interlude 1	Hey, hey. Hey, hey.
	Hey, hey. Hey, hey.
	A
	Hey, hey. Hey, hey.
	E
	Hey, hey. Hey, hey. Come to me now.
	B7 **A**
	Hey, hey. Hey, hey. Gonna get ya.
	E
	Hey, hey. Well, I'll tell ya.

Verse 3	**E** Now, I love this girl, I said, uh, Ruby is her name. Ah.

Believe me now.

When this girl looks at me she just sets my soul aflame.

Don't you know?

Chorus 3   **A**
Whoa, ____ I got some hugs and, uh, kisses too, yeah.

E
Now, I'm gonna give, uh, them, uh, all to you.

              B7   **A**   **E**
Now, listen, now,   Ruby, Ruby, when will you be mine?

I'm gonna get you sometime, Ruby, uh.

Interlude 2   *Repeat Interlude 1 w/ vocal ad lib.*

Outro   **E**
Ruby, Ruby, Ruby, Ruby, will you be mine?

Ah, your time. Ev'rybody, uh.   ***Fade out***

See You Later, Alligator

Words and Music by
Robert Guidry

Melody:

Well, I   saw my   ba - by   walk - in'

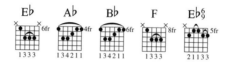

Eb	Ab	Bb	F	Eb6/9
6fr	4fr	6fr	8fr	5fr
1 3 3 3	1 3 4 2 1 1	1 3 4 2 1 1	1 3 3 3	2 1 1 3 3

Intro
      N.C.
      (See you later, alligator.)

Verse 1
            Eb
      Well, I saw my baby walkin' with another man today.

           Ab   **Eb**
      Well, I saw my baby walkin' with another man to - day.

                   Bb   **Eb**
      When I ask her, "What's the matter?" This is what I heard her say.

Chorus 1
      N.C.   **Eb**
      "See you later, alli - gator. After while, crocodile.

           Ab   **Eb**
      See you later, alli - gator. After while, croco - dile.

                  Bb
      Can't you see you're in my way now?

                  Eb
      Don't you know you cramp my style?"

Verse 2

      N.C.   E♭
When I thought of what she told me, nearly made me lose my head.

                    A♭   E♭
When I thought of what she told me, nearly made me lose my head.

                 B♭   E♭
But the next time that I saw her, reminded her of what she said.

Chorus 2   *Repeat Chorus 1*

Interlude

E♭				
A♭		E♭		
A♭		E♭	N.C.	

Verse 3

                    E♭
She said, "I'm sorry, pretty daddy, you know my love is just for you."

                    A♭   E♭
She said, "I'm sorry, pretty daddy, you know my love is just for you.

                 B♭
Won't you say that you'll for - give me

              E♭
And say your love for me is true?"

Verse 4

      N.C.   E♭
   I said, "Wait a minute, 'gator, I know you mean it just for play."

                 A♭   E♭
I said, "Wait a minute, 'gator, I know you mean it just for play."

                 B♭   E♭
Don't you know you really hurt me? And this is what I have to say.

Chorus 3   *Repeat Chorus 1*

Outro-Chorus

      N.C.   E♭
   See you later, alli - gator. After while, crocodile.

                 A♭   F   B♭   E♭§
See you later, alli - gator. So long. ___ That's all. ___ Goodbye.

Sh-Boom
(Life Could Be a Dream)

Words and Music by James Keyes,
Claude Feaster, Carl Feaster,
Floyd McRae and James Edwards

Melody:

Hey-non-ny, ding dong,   a - lang, a-lang, a - lang.

F   Dm   Gm7   C7   A7   D7   G7

134211   231   131111   13141   1 2   213   131211

Intro
F   Dm   Gm7   C7
Heynonny, ding dong, a - lang, alang, a - lang.

F   Dm   Gm7   C7
Boom, ba - doh, ba - doo, badoo, ba - lay.

Verse 1
F   Dm   Gm7   C7
Oh, life could be a dream,   if I could take you up in

F   Dm Gm7   C7
Paradise up a - bove,   if you would tell me I'm the

F   Dm   Gm7   C7   F
Only one that you love, life could be a dream, sweet - heart.

Dm   Gm7   C7
Hello, hel - lo again, sh - boom, I'm hopin' we'll meet again.

Verse 2
F   Dm   Gm7   C7
Oh, life could be a dream,   if only all my

F   Dm Gm7   C7
Precious plans would come true,   if you would let me

F   Dm Gm7   C7   F
Spend my whole life loving you, life could be a dream, sweet - heart.

Bridge 1

A7　　　　　　　　　　　D7
Now ev'ry time I look at you something is on my mind.

G7　　　　　　　Gm7　　　　C7
If you do what I want you to, baby, we'd be so fine.

Verse 3

　　　　F　　　　　Dm　Gm7　　　C7
Oh, life could be a dream,　　if I could take you up in

F　　　　　Dm　Gm7　　　C7
Paradise up a - bove,　　if you would tell me I'm the

F　　　　　　Dm　Gm7　　　C7　　　　　F
Only one that you love, life could be a dream, sweet - heart.

Chorus 1

　　　　F　　　Dm　Gm7　　　　　C7
Sh - boom, sh - boom, ya, da, da, da, da, da, da, da, da, da.

F　　　Dm　Gm7　　　　　C7
Sh - boom, sh - boom, ya, da, da, da, da, da, da, da, da, da.

F　　　Dm　Gm7　　　　　C7　　　　　F　　N.C.
Sh - boom, sh - boom, ya, da, da, da, da, da, da, da, da, sh - boom.

Chorus 2　Repeat Chorus 1

Bridge 2　Repeat Bridge 1

Verse 4　Repeat Verse 1

Interlude

F　　　　Dm　　　　Gm7　　　C7
　Heynonny, ding dong, a - lang, alang, a - lang.

F　　　Dm　　Gm7　　　C7
Boom, ba - doh, ba - doo, badoo, ba - lay.

F　　　Dm　　Gm7　　　C7　　　　F
Life could be a dream, life could be a dream, sweet - heart.

Verse 5　Repeat Verse 2

Outro

　　　F　　Dm　　Gm7　　C7
‖: 　(Doo, doo, sh - boom, sh - boom.)　:‖　　*Play 3 times*

N.C.　　F
Sweetheart.

Sherry

Words and Music by
Bob Gaudio

Melody:

Sher - ry, Sher-ry ba - by.

C   Am   Dm7   G7   C*   E♭   F   E7   A7   D7

Intro

‖: C   Am |Dm7 G7 :‖

C   Am Dm7   G7
Sher - ry,   Sherry, baby.

C   Am Dm7   G7
Sher - ry,   Sherry, baby.

Chorus 1

C Am Dm7 G7   C   Am Dm7   G7
Sher   -   ry, ba - by.   (Sherry, baby.)

C Am Dm7   G7   C
Sher - ry, ____ can you come out to - night?

        Am   Dm7   G7
(Come, come, come out to - night.)

Chorus 2

C Am Dm7 G7   C   Am Dm7   G7
Sher   -   ry, ba - by.   (Sherry, baby.)

C Am Dm7   G7   C*   E♭ F C* N.C.
Sher - ry, ____ can you come out to - night?

Verse 1

            E7
(Why don't you come on, come on) To my twist party?

    A7
(Come on.) Where the bright moon shines.

    D7
(Come on.) We'll dance the night away.

G7 N.C.
I'm gonna make you mi-yi-yi-yine.

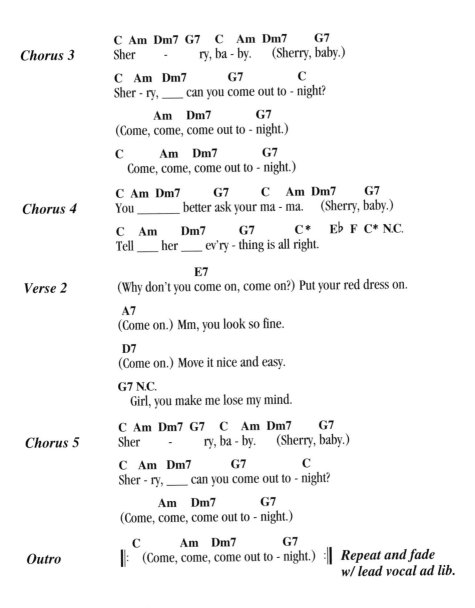

Chorus 3

C Am Dm7 G7   C   Am Dm7   G7
Sher   -   ry, ba - by.   (Sherry, baby.)

C   Am Dm7   G7   C
Sher - ry, ____ can you come out to - night?

          Am   Dm7   G7
(Come, come, come out to - night.)

C   Am   Dm7   G7
   Come, come, come out to - night.)

Chorus 4

C Am Dm7   G7   C   Am Dm7   G7
You _____ better ask your ma - ma.   (Sherry, baby.)

C   Am   Dm7   G7   C*   E♭ F C* N.C.
Tell ___ her ___ ev'ry - thing is all right.

Verse 2

                          E7
(Why don't you come on, come on?) Put your red dress on.

A7
(Come on.) Mm, you look so fine.

D7
(Come on.) Move it nice and easy.

G7 N.C.
   Girl, you make me lose my mind.

Chorus 5

C Am Dm7 G7   C   Am Dm7   G7
Sher   -   ry, ba - by.   (Sherry, baby.)

C Am Dm7   G7   C
Sher - ry, ____ can you come out to - night?

          Am   Dm7   G7
(Come, come, come out to - night.)

Outro

          C   Am   Dm7   G7
‖: (Come, come, come out to - night.) :‖ *Repeat and fade*
                                           w/ lead vocal ad lib.

Shop Around

Words and Music by Berry Gordy
and William "Smokey" Robinson

Melody:

When I be-came of age, my moth-er called me to her side.

G   C   A7   D7   G7   C7

Intro

G
When I became of age, my mother called me to her side.   C

A7
She said, "Son, you're growing up now, pretty soon you'll take a bride."   D7

Verse 1

G7
And then she said, "Just because you've be - come a young man now,   C7

G7   C7
There's still some things that you don't understand now.

G7   C7
Before you ask some girl for her hand now,

G7   C7
Keep your freedom for as long as you can now."

A7   D7 N.C.   G7
My mama told me you better shop a - round,

    C7   G7   D7
Oh, yeah, you better shop a - round.

Verse 2

G7   C7
Ah, ___ there's some things that I want you to know now.

G7   C7
A, just as sure as the wind's gonna blow now,

G7   C7
The women come and the women gonna go now.

G7   C7
Before you tell 'em that you love 'em so now,

A7   D7 N.C.   G7
My mama told me you better shop a - round,

    C7   G7   D7
Oh, yeah, you better shop a - round.

Bridge 1

C7
A, try to get yourself a bargain, son.

G7
Don't ___ be sold on the very first one.

C7
A, pretty girls come a dime a dozen.

D7 N.C.   D7 N.C.
A, try to find one who's gonna give you true lovin'.

Verse 3

G7   C7
Before you take a girl and say I do now,

G7   C7
A, make sure she's in love with a you now.

A7   D7 N.C.   G7 N.C. G7 N.C.
My mama told me you better shop a - round.

Sax Solo

| G7 | C7 | G7 | C7 | |
| G7 | C7 | G7 N.C. | | |

Bridge 2   *Repeat Bridge 1*

Verse 4

G7   C7
Before you take a girl and say I do now,

G7   C7
Make sure she's in love with you now.

G7   C7
Make sure that her love is true now,

G7   C7
I hate to see you feelin' sad and blue now.

A7   D7 N.C.   G7
My mama told me you better shop a - round.

Outro

          C7   G7
‖: Ah huh, don't let the first one get ya.

            C7   G7
Oh, no, ___ 'cause I don't wanna see 'em with ya,

        C7   G7
Ah huh, before you let 'em hold ___ you tight. :‖ ***Repeat and fade***
                                                     w/ vocal ad lib.

Since I Don't Have You

Words and Music by James Beaumont,
Janet Vogel, Joseph Verscharen,
Walter Lester, Lennie Martin,
Joseph Rock and John Taylor

Melody:

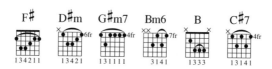

I _____ don't have __ plans and schemes. _

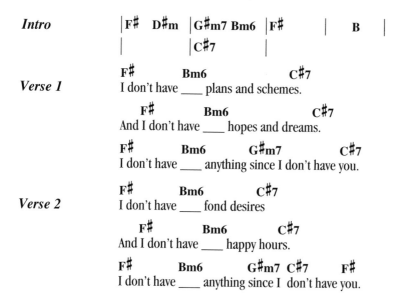

Intro

|F♯   D♯m |G♯m7 Bm6 |F♯ | B |
| |C♯7 |

Verse 1

F♯   Bm6   C♯7
I don't have ___ plans and schemes.

F♯   Bm6   C♯7
And I don't have ___ hopes and dreams.

F♯   Bm6   G♯m7   C♯7
I don't have ___ anything since I don't have you.

Verse 2

F♯   Bm6   C♯7
I don't have ___ fond desires

F♯   Bm6   C♯7
And I don't have ___ happy hours.

F♯   Bm6   G♯m7 C♯7   F♯
I don't have ___ anything since I don't have you.

Bridge

G#m7   F#
I don't have ___ happiness and I guess

G#m7   F#
I never will ever a - gain.

G#m7   F#
When you walked out on me   in walked the misery,

G#m7   C#7
And he's been here since then.

Verse 3

    F#   Bm6   C#7
I ___ don't have ___ love to share,

    F#   Bm6   C#7
And I don't have ___ one who cares.

F#   Bm6
I don't have ___ anything

G#m7   C#7   F#   D#m   G#m7   C#7
Since I   don't have   you,   you,   you,   you.

Outro

    F#   D#m   G#m7   C#7
‖: You,   you,   you,   you. :‖

F#
  You.

Sixteen Reasons
(Why I Love You)

Words and Music by
Bill Post and Doree Post

(Six - teen rea - sons) Why _ I love

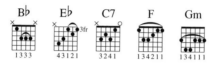

Intro

| Bb | Eb | | Bb C7 | F |

(Sixteen reasons) Why I love you.

Verse 1

Bb   Gm
(One,) The way you hold my hand,

Eb   F
(Two,) Your laugh - ing eyes,

Bb   Gm
(Three,) The way ___ you understand,

Eb   F
(Four,) Your se - cret sighs,

Bb   Gm   Eb   F
They're all ___ a part of six - teen reasons

Bb C7   F
Why I love you.

Verse 2

Bb   Gm
(Five,) The way you comb your hair,

Eb   F
(Six,) Your freckled nose,

Bb   Gm
(Seven,) The way ____ you say you care,

Eb   F
(Eight,) Your cra - zy clothes,

Bb   Gm   Eb   F
   That's just ____ half of sixteen ____ reasons

   Bb C7   F   Bb
Why I   love ____ you.

Bridge

Eb
(Nine,) Snuggling in the car,

Bb
(Ten,) Your wish upon a star,

  C7
(E - leven,) Whisp'ring on the phone,

F
(Twelve,) Your kiss when we're alone.

Verse 3

     Bb   Gm
(Thir - teen,) The way ____ you thrill my heart,

     Eb   F
(Four - teen,) Your voice ____ so neat,

    Bb   Gm
(Fif - teen,) You say we'll never part,

    Eb   F
(Six - teen,) Our love's ____ complete.

Bb   Gm   Eb   F   Bb C7   F Bb Eb
Those are all of ____ sixteen reasons, why I   love ____ you.

Bb   Eb   Bb C7   F   Bb
(Sixteen reasons) Why I   love ____ you.

The Stroll

Words and Music by
Clyde Otis and Nancy Lee

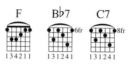

Intro | F | | | | |

Verse 1

F
Come, let's stroll, stroll across the floor.

Bb7   **F**
Come, let stroll, stroll across the floor.

   C7   **Bb7**   **F**
Now turn around, baby,   let's stroll once more.

Verse 2

F
Feel so good, take me by my hand.

 Bb7   **F**
I feel so good, take me by my hand.

   C7   **Bb7**   **F**
And let's go strolling   in wonderland.

Chorus

F
Strolling, whoa, yeah. Strolling, ah huh.

     Bb7   **F**
Rock and rolling, strolling.

     C7   **Bb7**   **F**
Well, a rock a my soul,   how I love to stroll.

Verse 3

F
There's my love, strolling in the door.

Bb7   **F**
There's my love, strolling in the door.

   C7   **Bb7**   **F**
Baby, let's go strolling   by the candy store.

Outro

Repeat Chorus 1 (Instrumental) till fade

Who Put the Bomp

(In the Bomp Ba Bomp Ba Bomp)

Words and Music by
Barry Mann and Gerry Goffin

I'd like to thank the guy _____ who wrote the

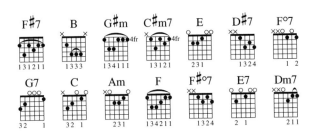

Intro

F#7   B   G#m
I'd like to thank the guy ___ who wrote the song

         C#m7   F#7
That made my baby fall in love with me.

| N.C. (Drums) | | |

Chorus 1

B   G#m
Who put the bomp in the bomp, ba, bomp, ba, bomp?

E   F#7
Who put the ram in the ram-a-lam-a-ding-dong?

B   G#m
Who put the bop in the bop, shbop, shbop?

E   F#7
Who put the dip in the dip, didip, didip?

B   D#7   E   F°7
Who was that man? I'd like to shake his hand.

B   G#m C#m7 F#7   B   F#7
He made my baby fall in love with me. (Yeah.)

Verse 1

     B   G#m
When my baby heard,

E   F#7
Bomp, ba-ba-bomp, ba - bom-ba-bomp-bomp,

B   G#m   E   F#7
Ev'ry word went right into her heart.

    B   G#m
And when she heard them singing,

E   F°7
Ram-a-lam-a-lam-a-lam-a-ding-dong,

B   G#m   C#m F#7   B   F#7
She said we'd never have to part.

Chorus 2

     B   G#m
So, who put the bomp in the bomp, ba, bomp, ba, bomp?

E   F#7
Who put the ram in the ram-a-lam-a-ding-dong?

B   G#m
Who put the bop in the bop, shbop, shbop?

E   F#7
Who put the dip in the dip, didip, didip?

B   D#7   E   F°7
Who was that man? I'd like to shake his hand.

   B   G#m C#m7 F#7   B   G7
He made my baby   fall in   love with me. (Yeah.)

Verse 2

        C   Am
Each time that we're a - lone,

F   G7
Boogadee, boogadee, boogadee, boogadee, boogadee, boogadee, shoe.

C   Am   F G7
Sets my baby's heart all a - glow.

     C   Am
And ev'ry time we dance to

F   F#°7
Dip, didip, didip didip, dip, didip, didip didip,

C Am   F   G7   C G7
She always says she loves me so.

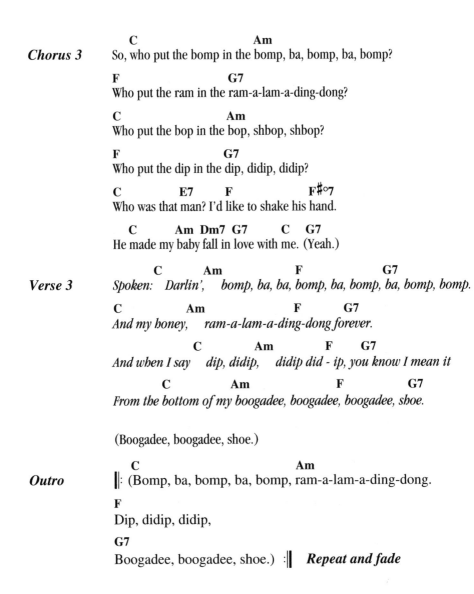

Chorus 3
C   Am
So, who put the bomp in the bomp, ba, bomp, ba, bomp?

F   G7
Who put the ram in the ram-a-lam-a-ding-dong?

C   Am
Who put the bop in the bop, shbop, shbop?

F   G7
Who put the dip in the dip, didip, didip?

C   E7 F   F$\sharp°7$
Who was that man? I'd like to shake his hand.

  C   Am Dm7 G7 C G7
He made my baby fall in love with me. (Yeah.)

Verse 3
     C   Am   F   G7
Spoken: Darlin', bomp, ba, ba, bomp, ba, bomp, ba, bomp, bomp.

C   Am   F   G7
And my honey, ram-a-lam-a-ding-dong forever.

       C   Am   F G7
And when I say dip, didip, didip did - ip, you know I mean it

      C   Am   F   G7
From the bottom of my boogadee, boogadee, boogadee, shoe.

(Boogadee, boogadee, shoe.)

Outro
    C   Am
‖: (Bomp, ba, bomp, ba, bomp, ram-a-lam-a-ding-dong.

F
Dip, didip, didip,

G7
Boogadee, boogadee, shoe.) :‖ ***Repeat and fade***

Stupid Cupid

Words and Music by
Howard Greenfield and Neil Sedaka

Stu - pid Cu - pid, you're a   real mean   guy, ____

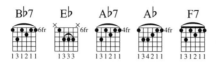

| Bb7 | Eb | Ab7 | Ab | F7 |

Intro | Bb7 |

Verse 1

Eb N.C.

Stupid Cupid, you're a real mean guy,

Eb

(Stupid Cupid.) I'd like to clip your wings so you can't fly.

Ab7

(Stupid Cupid.) I'm in love and it's a cryin' shame,

Eb

(Stupid Cupid.) And I know that you're the one to blame.

Bb7   Ab7

(Stupid Cupid.) Hey, hey, set me free.

Eb N.C.

Stupid Cupid, stop pickin' on me.

Verse 2

Eb

I can't do my homework and I can't think straight.

(Stupid Cupid.) I meet him ev'ry mornin' about a half past eight.

Ab7

(Stupid Cupid.) I'm actin' like a love sick fool.

Eb

(Stupid Cupid.) He's even got me carryin' his books to school.

Bb7   Ab7

(Stupid Cupid.) Hey, hey, set me free.

Eb N.C.

Stupid Cupid, stop pickin' on me.

Bridge

A♭   E♭

You mixed me up, but good, right from the very start.

A♭   F7 N.C.   F7 N.C. B♭7

Hey, go play Robin Hood with, with somebody else's   heart.

Verse 3

E♭

You got me jumpin' like a crazy clown,

(Stupid Cupid.) And I don't feature what you're puttin' down.

A♭7

(Stupid Cupid.) Since I kissed his lovin' lips of wine,

E♭

(Stupid Cupid.) The thing that bothers me is that I like it fine.

B♭7   A♭7

(Stupid Cupid.) Hey, hey, set me free.

E♭ N.C.

Stupid Cupid, stop pickin' on me.

Sax Solo   *Repeat Bridge (Instrumental)*

Verse 4

E♭ N.C.

You got me jumpin' like a crazy clown,

E♭

(Stupid Cupid.) And I don't feature what you're puttin' down.

A♭7

(Stupid Cupid.) Since I kissed his lovin' lips of wine,

E♭

(Stupid Cupid.) The thing that bothers me is that I like it fine.

B♭7   A♭7

(Stupid Cupid.) Hey, hey, set me free.

E♭ N.C.

Stupid Cupid, stop pickin' on me.

B♭7   A♭7

Hey, hey, set me free.

E♭ N.C.

Stupid Cupid, stop pickin' on me.

Outro

E♭

‖: (Stupid Cupid. Stupid Cupid.) :‖   ***Repeat and fade***

Sweet Nothin's

Words and Music by
Ronnie Self

Melody:

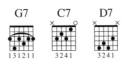

My ba - by whis-pers in my   ear. __

G7   C7   D7

131211   3241   3241

Verse 1

    G7 N.C.   G7   C7   G7
    My baby whispers in my ear. Mm, ___ sweet noth - in'.

                                        C7   G7
He knows the things I like to hear. Mm, ___ sweet noth - in'.

C7
Things he wouldn't tell nobody else.

G7 N.C.
Secret, baby, I keep 'em to myself.

              D7   C7   G7
Sweet noth - in'. Mm, ___ sweet noth - in'.

Verse 2

    N.C.   G7   C7   G7
    We walk along hand-in-hand. Mm, ___ sweet noth - in'.

                                  C7   G7
Yeah, we both understand. Mm, ___ sweet noth - in'.

C7
Sittin' in class, I'm tryin' to read my book,

G7 N.C.
My baby give me that special look.

              D7   C7   G7
Sweet noth - in'. Mm, ___ sweet noth - in'.

Sax Solo   ‖: G7 | C7 | G7 | | :‖
            | C7 | | G7 | |
            | D7 | C7 | G7 | N.C. |

Verse 3

                           G7   **C7**   **G7**
I'm sittin' on my front porch. Mm, ____ sweet noth - in'.

                                   C7   **G7**
Well, do I love you? Of course. Mm, ____ sweet noth - in'.

C7
Mama turned off the front porch light and said,

G7 N.C.
   "Come in, darlin', that's enough for tonight."

              D7   **C7**   **G7**
Sweet noth - in'. Mm, ____ sweet noth - in'.

              D7   **C7**   **G7**   **N.C.**
Sweet noth - in'. Mm, ____ sweet noth - in'.

                 G7
Sweet nothin's.

Tell Laura I Love Her

Words and Music by
Jeff Barry and Ben Raleigh

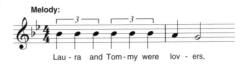

Melody:

Lau - ra and Tom - my were lov - ers,

(Capo 6th fret)

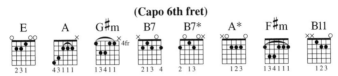

E   A   G#m   B7   B7*   A*   F#m   B11

Verse 1

         E   A
        Laura and Tommy were lovers,

       E   A
He wanted to give her ev'ry - thing.

       G#m   A   B7   B7*
Flowers,   presents,   and most of all,   a wedding ring.

   E   A*
   He saw a sign for a stock car race,

 G#m   A
   A thousand dollar prize, ___ it read.

 G#m   A
   He couldn't get Laura on the phone,

  B7
So to her mother Tommy said,

Chorus 1

   E
   "Tell Laura I love her.

   F#m
Tell Laura I need her.

     E
Tell Laura I may be late,

  A*   E
I've something to do that cannot wait."

Verse 2

E   A*
He drove his car to the racing grounds,

E   A*
He was the youngest driver there.

G#m   A
The crowd roared as they started the race,

        B7
'Round the track they drove at a deadly pace.

E   A*
No one knows what happened that day,

E   A*
How his car over - turned in flames.

   G#m   A
But as they pulled him from the twisted wreck,

     B7
With his dying breath, they heard him say,

Chorus 2

E
"Tell Laura I love her.

        F#m
Tell Laura I need her.

       E
Tell Laura not to cry,

    A   B11   E11
My love for her will nev - er die."

Verse 3

E   A*
Now, in the chapel   where Laura prays

E   A*
For her Tommy who passed away,

G#m   A
It was just for Laura he lived and died,

    B7
Alone ___ in the chapel she can hear him cry.

Chorus 3   *Repeat Chorus 2*

Outro

                 E
‖: (Boom, boom, boom, boom.)

Tell Laura I love her. :‖   ***Repeat and fade***

Venus

Words and Music by
Edward Marshall

Hey, __ Ve - nus, ____ oh,

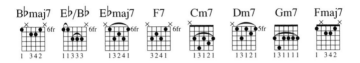

B♭maj7   E♭/B♭   E♭maj7   F7   Cm7   Dm7   Gm7   Fmaj7

Intro

‖: **B♭maj7** | **E♭/B♭** :‖

B♭maj7   E♭maj7   F7
Hey, Venus, oh, Venus.

Verse 1

    B♭maj7   **Cm7**   **B♭maj7**
Venus, if you will,   please send a little girl for me to thrill.

    Cm7   **Dm7**
  A girl who wants my kisses and my arms,

     Cm7   **F7**   **B♭maj7   E♭/B♭**
A girl with all the charms of you.

Verse 2

    B♭maj7   **Cm7**   **B♭maj7**
Venus, make her fair,   a lovely girl with sunlight in her hair.

    Cm7   **Dm7**
  And take the brightest stars up in the skies

     Cm7   **F7**   **B♭maj7   E♭/B♭**
And place them in her eyes for me.

Chorus 1

Ebmaj7	Cm7	F7	Bbmaj7

Venus,   goddess of love that you are,

Gm7   Fmaj7
Surely the things I ask

Gm7   Cm7 F7
Can't be too great a task.

Verse 3

Bbmaj7   Cm7   Bbmaj7
Venus, if you do,   I promise that I always will be true.

Cm7   Dm7
I'll give her all the love I have to give

Cm7   F7   Bbmaj7 Eb/Bb
As long as we both shall live.

Chorus 2   *Repeat Chorus 1*

Verse 4   *Repeat Verse 3*

Outro

Bbmaj7   Ebmaj7 F7 N.C.
Hey, Venus, oh, Venus,

F7   Bbmaj7 Eb/Bb Bbmaj7 Eb/Bb Bbmaj7
Make my wish come true.

Walk Right In

Words and Music by
Gus Cannon and H. Woods

Melody:

Walk right in,   set right _ down. _

Tune down 1/2 step:
(low to high) Eb - Ab - Db - Gb - Bb - Eb

A	F#7	B7	E	D7	D7/F#
1 2 3	1 3 1 2 1 1	2 1 3 4	2 3 1	2 1 3	T 2 1 3

Intro

A		F#7	B7 E	A	
		F#7	B7	E	
A			N.C. (D7)	D7/F#	
A		F#7	B7 E	A	

Verse 1

  A   F#7
Walk right in, set right down.

B7   E   A
Daddy, let your mind roll on.

                F#7
Walk right in, set right down.

B7   E
Daddy, let your mind roll on.

A
Ev'rybody's talkin' 'bout a new way of walkin'.

N.C.(D7)   D7/F#
Do you wanna lose your mind?

A   F#7
Walk right in, set right down.

B7   E   A
Daddy, let your mind roll on.

Verse 2

A   F#7
Walk right in, set right down.

B7   E   A
Baby, let your hair hang down.

               F#7
Walk right in, set right down.

B7   E
Baby, let your hair hang down.

A
Ev'rybody's talkin' 'bout a new way of walkin.'

N.C. (D7)   D7/F#
Do you wanna lose your mind?

A   F#7
Walk right in, set right down.

B7   E   A
Baby, let your hair hang down.

Interlude

Repeat Intro

Verse 3

A   F#7
Walk right in, set right down.

B7   E   A
Daddy, let your mind roll on.

               F#7
Walk right in, set right down.

B7   E
Daddy, let your mind roll on.

A
Ev'rybody's talkin' 'bout a new way of walkin'.

N.C.(D7)   D7/F#
Do you wanna lose your mind?

A   F#7
Walk right in, set right down.

B7   E   A F#7
Daddy, let your mind roll on.

B7   E   A
Daddy, let your mind roll on.

Where Have All the Flowers Gone?

Words and Music by
Pete Seeger

Melody:

Where have all the flow-ers gone? __

(Capo 3rd fret)

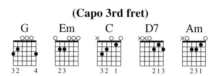

G   Em   C   D7   Am

Intro | G   Em | C   D7 |

Verse 1
G   Em   C   D7
Where have all the flowers gone?   Long time passing.

G   Em   C   D7
Where have all the flowers gone? ____ Long time a - go.

G   Em   C   D7
Where have all the flowers gone? Young girls picked them, ev'ry one.

Am   G   C   D7 G   D7
When will they ever learn?   When will they ever learn?

Verse 2
G   Em   C   D7
Where have all the young girls gone?   Long time passing.

G   Em   C   D7
Where have all the young girls gone? ____ Long time a - go.

G   Em   C   D7
Where have all the young girls gone? Gone to young men, ev'ry one.

Am   G   C   D7 G   D7
When will they ever learn?   When will they ever learn?

Verse 3

G   Em   C   D7
Where have all the young men gone?   Long time passing.

G   Em   C   D7
Where have all the young men gone? ___ Long time a - go.

G   Em   C   D7
Where have all the young men gone? Gone for soldiers, ev'ry one.

Am   G   C   D7 G   D7
When will they ever learn?   When will they ever learn?

Verse 4

G   Em   C   D7
Where have all the soldiers gone?   Long time passing.

G   Em   C   D7
Where have all the soldiers gone? A long, long time a - go.

G   Em   C   D7
Where have all the soldiers gone? Gone to graveyards, ev'ry one.

Am   G   C   D7 G   D7
When will they ever learn?   When will they ever learn?

Verse 5

G   Em   C   D7
Where have all the graveyards gone?   Long time passing.

G   Em   C   D7
Where have all the graveyards gone? ___ Long time a - go.

G   Em   C   D7   N.C.
Where have all the graveyards gone? Gone to flowers, ev'ry one.

               G   C   D7 G   D7 G D7 G
When will they ever learn?   When will they ever learn?

A White Sport Coat
(And a Pink Carnation)

Words and Music by
Marty Robbins

Melody:

A white sport coat

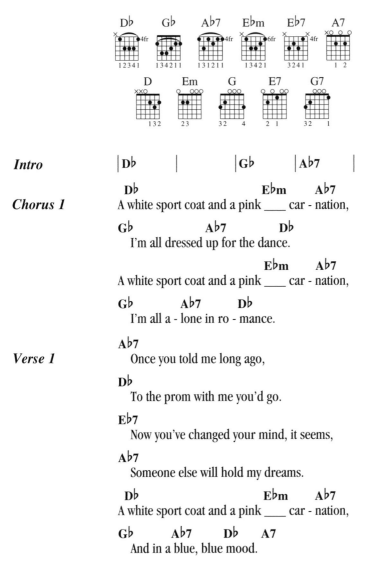

Intro | Db | | Gb | Ab7 |

Chorus 1
```
      Db                  Ebm      Ab7
A white sport coat and a pink ____ car - nation,

Gb          Ab7         Db
I'm all dressed up for the dance.

                   Ebm      Ab7
A white sport coat and a pink ____ car - nation,

Gb        Ab7     Db
I'm all a - lone in ro - mance.
```

Verse 1
```
Ab7
   Once you told me long ago,

Db
   To the prom with me you'd go.

Eb7
   Now you've changed your mind, it seems,

Ab7
   Someone else will hold my dreams.

  Db                  Ebm      Ab7
A white sport coat and a pink ____ car - nation,

Gb      Ab7     Db    A7
And in a blue, blue mood.
```

	D Em A7

Chorus 2

       D   **Em**   **A7**
(A white sport coat and a pink ___ car - nation.)

G   **A7**   **D**
I'm all dressed up for the dance.

                                   Em   **A7**
(A white sport coat and a pink ___ car - nation.)

G   **A7**   **D**
I'm all a - lone in ro - mance.

Verse 2

A7
Once you told me long ago,

D
To the prom with me you'd go.

E7
Now you've changed your mind it seems,

A7
Someone else will hold my dreams.

    D   **Em**   **A7**
A white sport coat and a pink ___ car - nation,

G   **A7**   **D**   **G7 D**
I'm in a blue, blue mood.

Will You Love Me Tomorrow

(Will You Still Love Me Tomorrow)

Words and Music by
Gerry Goffin and Carole King

Melody:

To - night _ you're mine _____ com - plete - ly. _

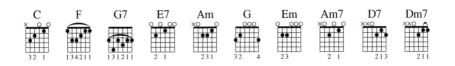

C   F   G7   E7   Am   G   Em   Am7   D7   Dm7

Intro

|C | | | |

Verse 1

   C   F   G7
Tonight you're mine com - pletely.

   C   G7
You give your love so sweetly.

        E7   Am
To - night, the light of love is in your eyes.

   F   G   C
But will you love me to - morrow?

Verse 2

   C   F   G7
Is this a lasting treasure,

   C   G7
Or just a moment's pleasure?

        E7   Am
Can I believe the magic of your sighs?

   F   G   C
Will you still love me to - morrow?

Bridge

F   Em
Tonight with words un - spoken

F   C
You say that I'm the only one.

F   Em
But will my heart be broken

          Am7
When the night, (When the night.)

          D7   Dm7 G7
Meets the morning (Meets the morning.) sun?

Verse 3

C   F   G7
I like to know that your love

C   G7
Is a love I can be sure of.

        E7   Am
So tell me now and I won't ask again.

F   G   C
Will you still love me to - morrow?

Interlude

| C | | F | | G7 | |
| C | | G7 | | |

Outro

        E7   Am
So tell me now and I won't ask again.

        F   G   C
‖: Will you still love me to - morrow? :‖ *Repeat and fade*

Young Blood

Words and Music by Jerry Leiber,
Mike Stoller and Doc Pomus

Melody:

I saw her stand-in' on the cor-ner,

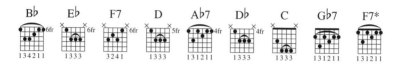

Bb   Eb   F7   D   Ab7   Db   C   Gb7   F7*

Verse 1

  Bb
I saw her standin' on the corner,

A yellow ribbon in her hair.

I couldn't keep myself from shoutin',
  N.C.
"Look a there, look a there, look a there, look a there."

Chorus 1

Eb **Bb**
Young blood, young blood,

Eb   **F7 N.C.**
Young blood, I can't get you outta my mind.

Verse 2

 Bb
I took one look and I was fractured.

I tried to walk but I was lame.

I tried to talk but I just stuttered,
  N.C.
"What's your name, what's your name,

What's your name, what's your name?"

Chorus 2	*Repeat Chorus 1*
Bridge	E♭ D E♭ What crazy stuff, she looked so tough.

A♭7
I had to follow her all the way home.

D♭   C D♭
 Then things went bad,   I met her dad.

          G♭7   F7*
He said,   "You better leave my daughter a - lone."

Verse 3	B♭ Well, I couldn't sleep a wink for tryin'.

I saw the rising of the sun.

And all night long my heart was cryin',

             N.C.
"You're the one, you're the one, you're the one, you're the one."

Chorus 3	*Repeat Chorus 1*
Chorus 4	E♭ B♭ Young blood, young blood,

E♭   F7 N.C.   B♭
Young blood, I can't get you outta my mind.

Guitar Chord Songbooks

Each book includes complete lyrics, chord symbols, and guitar chord diagrams.

Acoustic Rock

A handy collection of 80 acoustic favorites: Angie • Blackbird • Blowin' in the Wind • Bridge over Troubled Water • Drive • Dust in the Wind • Fast Car • Here Comes the Sun • If You Could Only See • Layla • Maggie May • Me and Julio down by the Schoolyard • Mrs. Robinson • Pink Houses • The Sound of Silence • Torn • Yesterday • and more.
00699540 . . . .$17.95

The Beatles (A-I)

An awesome reference of Beatles hits: All You Need Is Love • And I Love Her • The Ballad of John and Yoko • Blackbird • Can't Buy Me Love • A Day in the Life • Eight Days a Week • Eleanor Rigby • Get Back • Good Day Sunshine • A Hard Day's Night • Help! • Here Comes the Sun • Hey Jude • I Saw Her Standing There • In My Life • and more!
00699558 . . . .$16.95

The Beatles (J-Y)

100 more Beatles hits: Lady Madonna • Let It Be • Love Me Do • Michelle • Norwegian Wood • Ob-La-Di, Ob-La-Da • Paperback Writer • Revolution • Sgt. Pepper's Lonely Hearts Club Band • Strawberry Fields Forever • Twist and Shout • We Can Work It Out • When I'm Sixty-Four • Yellow Submarine • Yesterday • and more.
00699562 . . . .$16.95

The Beach Boys

59 favorites: Barbara Ann • Be True to Your School • California Girls • Catch a Wave • Don't Worry Baby • Fun, Fun, Fun • Good Vibrations • Help Me Rhonda • I Get Around • In My Room • Kokomo • Little Deuce Coupe • Surfin' U.S.A. • Wild Honey • Wouldn't It Be Nice • dozens more!
00699566 . . . .$14.95

Children's Songs

70 songs for kids: Alphabet Song • The Bear Went over the Mountain • Bingo • The Candy Man • Eensy Weensy Spider • It's a Small World • Mickey Mouse March • Old MacDonald • On Top of Spaghetti • Puff the Magic Dragon • Supercalifragilisticexpialidocious • Twinkle, Twinkle Little Star • Won't You Be My Neighbor? (It's a Beautiful Day in This Neighborhood) • and more!
00699539 . . . .$12.95

Christmas Carols

80 Christmas carols: Angels We Have Heard on High • Away in a Manger • Coventry Carol • Deck the Hall • Fum, Fum, Fum • Good King Wenceslas • The Holly and the Ivy • I Saw Three Ships • Joy to the World • O Holy Night • Silent Night • Up on the Housetop • We Wish You a Merry Christmas • What Child Is This? • and more.
00699536 . . . .$12.95

Johnny Cash

58 Cash classics: A Boy Named Sue • Cry, Cry, Cry • Daddy Sang Bass • Folsom Prison Blues • I Walk the Line • The Long Black Veil • The Man in Black • Orange Blossom Special • (Ghost) Riders in the Sky • Ring of Fire • Solitary Man • Tennessee Flat Top Box • You Win Again • and more.
00699648 . . . .$14.95

Christmas Songs

80 Christmas favorites: The Christmas Song • Feliz Navidad • Grandma Got Run over by a Reindeer • I Heard the Bells on Christmas Day • Jingle-Bell Rock • Merry Christmas, Darling • Rudolph the Red-Nosed Reindeer • Silver Bells • We Need a Little Christmas • more.
00699537 . . . .$12.95

Eric Clapton

75 of Slowhand's finest: Born Under a Bad Sign • Change the World • Have You Ever Loved a Woman • I Shot the Sheriff • Knockin' on Heaven's Door • Layla • Riding with the King • Strange Brew • Tears in Heaven • Wonderful Tonight • and more!
00699567 . . . .$14.95

Classic Rock

80 rock essentials: Beast of Burden • Cat Scratch Fever • Free Ride • Hot Blooded • Layla • Money • Owner of a Lonely Heart • Rhiannon • Start Me Up • Sweet Emotion • Take Me to the River • Walk on the Wild Side • and more
00699598 . . . .$12.95

Contemporary Christian

80 hits from today's top CCM artists: Awesome God • Don't Look at Me • El Shaddai • Friends • The Great Divide • His Strength Is Perfect • I Will Be Here • Just One • Live Out Loud • A Maze of Grace • Oh Lord, You're Beautiful • Run to You • Speechless • Testify to Love • Via Dolorosa • more.
00699564 . . . .$14.95

Country

80 country standards: Always on My Mind • Boot Scootin' Boogie • Crazy • Elvira • Folsom Prison Blues • Hey, Good Lookin' • I Feel Lucky • Okie from Muskogee • Ring of Fire • Sixteen Tons • Through the Years • Your Cheatin' Heart • more.
00699534 . . . .$14.95

Cowboy Songs

Over 60 tunes: Back in the Saddle Again • Git Along, Little Dogies • Happy Trails • Home on the Range • Mexicali Rose • The Red River Valley • Sioux City Sue • Streets of Laredo • The Yellow Rose of Texas • and more.
00699636 . . . .$12.95

Folk Pop Rock

80 songs: American Pie • Constant Craving • Dust in the Wind • Here Comes the Sun • Me and Bobby McGee • Nights in White Satin • Somebody to Love • Time in a Bottle • Vincent (Starry Starry Night) • You Were Meant for Me • and more.
00699651 . . . .$12.95

 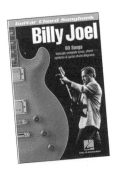 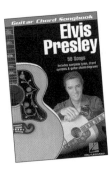 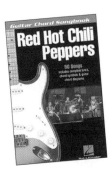

Folksongs

80 folk favorites: Aura Lee • Camptown Races • Danny Boy • Git Along, Little Dogies • Home on the Range • I've Been Working on the Railroad • Man of Constant Sorrow • Matilda • Nobody Knows the Trouble I've Seen • Scarborough Fair • When the Saints Go Marching In • and more.
00699541 . . . .$12.95

Billy Joel

60 Billy Joel favorites: Allentown • Honesty • It's Still Rock and Roll to Me • Just the Way You Are • Keeping the Faith • The Longest Time • My Life • New York State of Mind • Piano Man • Pressure • She's Always a Woman • Uptown Girl • We Didn't Start the Fire • You May Be Right • and more.
00699632 . . . .$14.95

Pop/Rock

80 chart hits: Against All Odds • All I Wanna Do • Closer to Free • Come Sail Away • Every Breath You Take • Give Me One Reason • Heartache Tonight • Hurts So Good • Imagine • Kokomo • Let It Be • More Than Words • Smooth • So Far Away • Summer of '69 • Twist and Shout • What I Like About You • Wonderful Tonight • and more.
00699538 . . . .$14.95

Elvis Presley

60 hits from The King: All Shook Up • Blue Suede Shoes • Can't Help Falling in Love • Don't Be Cruel (To a Heart That's True) • Heartbreak Hotel • Hound Dog • It's Now or Never • Jailhouse Rock • Love Me Tender • Return to Sender • Suspicious Minds • That's All Right • Viva Las Vegas • more.
00699633 . . . .$14.95

Red Hot Chili Peppers

50 hits from the Chili Peppers: Blood Sugar Sex Magik • Breaking the Girl • By the Way • Californication • Can't Stop • Get on Top • Give It Away • Higher Ground • Knock Me Down • Love Rollercoaster • One Hot Minute • Out in L.A. • Save the Population • Scar Tissue • Suck My Kiss • Under the Bridge • What It Is • and more.
00699710 . . . .$16.95

Rock 'n' Roll

80 rock 'n' roll classics: At the Hop • Barbara Ann • Chantilly Lace • Crying • Duke of Earl • Great Balls of Fire • I Get Around • It's My Party • La Bamba • Long Tall Sally • The Loco-Motion • My Boyfriend's Back • Peggy Sue • Return to Sender • Rock Around the Clock • Stand by Me • Surfin' U.S.A. • Willie and the Hand Jive • and more.
00699535 . . . .$12.95

Complete contents listings available online at www.halleonard.com

FOR MORE INFORMATION, SEE YOUR LOCAL MUSIC DEALER, OR WRITE TO:

HAL•LEONARD®
CORPORATION
7777 W. BLUEMOUND RD. P.O. BOX 13819 MILWAUKEE, WI 53213

www.halleonard.com

Prices, contents, and availability subject to change without notice.

1006